Now is the Time to Worship

Pursuing the Presence of God

By Rebecca Hossum

Published in the United States of America
Copyright © 2016 by Rebecca Hossum
All rights reserved.
ISBN-10: 0692706224
First Edition Printing
August 2016

ISBN-13: 978-0692706220
Vision Directives

Cover design by MinorDesignCo, LLC

Dedicated to the Body of Christ!

Contents

Acknowledgements

This book took seven years to write and would not have been possible without three very special people; Teresa Franklyn; my pseudo editor, Janelle Wright Middleton; my publisher, and Shelley Ann Tabor; my proofreader. You three ladies were like angels in disguise throughout this entire project, and I am eternally grateful for your time, support, and love.

Teresa, I have admired your writing since the day we met and considered your talent to be in a class of its own. This project might not have gotten off the ground if you did not say yes when I asked for your help. Your initial reaction to the first chapters of this book became the fuel that got me to the finish line. When an experienced, accomplished writer such as you, gives my work the stamp of approval, it's a gift that only fellow writers can understand. Thank you for your heartfelt encouraging feedback, it changed my concept of who I am as a writer.

Janelle, thank you for helping me bring my vision to life. I am truly honored to have you backing this project because you are a multi-talented force which is about to take this world by storm. Your creative genius, coupled with your brilliant mind will help take this book as far as God wants it to go. Being a writer yourself, you knew enough about the process to help keep me on track. At times when I lost focus, you always knew whether I needed tough love or motivation to help get me back on course. It is an invaluable gift when you have a friend who tells you what you *need* to hear and not what you *want* to hear. Thank you for being a friend.

Shelley, you held my feet to the fire and would not let me settle for mediocre when you knew I was capable of more. Thank you for being candid and honest with me about my writing, and for sending me back to the drawing board when certain pages fell short of the standard you came to expect from me.

To my Mom and Dad; you were the first to introduce me to Jesus Christ and that introduction shaped my life and led me to where I am today. I'm standing on a firm foundation in Christ because of the seeds you sowed into my life during those formative years. Our family life was far from perfect, but you kept God at the center of our home, and that made all the difference. I'm immensely proud to have come through your lineage, and I'll forever be grateful that God picked you both to be my parents.

To my Siblings; we are a colorful, unconventional bunch, but I wouldn't have it any other way. Thank you for always supporting my writing!

To Pastor Mary Cooper and the ladies of the Daughters of Esther ministry; Pastor Mary, thank you for being a woman of integrity and virtue, it has set you apart and made you worthy of emulating. The 10 years I spent with the ministry left a mark on my life that will never go away. A million thanks to you and the ladies, for your prayers and for laboring with me to see my God-given destiny come to fruition.

To my circle of close friends… you know who you are. Thank you for your unwavering support throughout this seven year journey, I could not have finished this book without your encouragement.

Lastly, Elizabeth Ann Haggar; you talked me off of the ledge more times than I can count. Whenever I became discouraged or tempted to throw in the towel, you found creative ways to reassure me that everything was going to work out. Thank you for responding to my endless stream of text messages, for assisting me with rewrites, and for putting together PowerPoint slides to help me see what the end product could look like. Words fall short as I attempt to express my gratitude for all that you've done. Thank you for being there for me; I am eternally grateful for your friendship!

Author's Preface

At the age of 8, my third-grade teacher, Mrs. Rodriguez, told me that I would one day write a book. While I don't remember a great deal about that time in my life, I very vividly remember the day when Mrs. Rodriguez spoke those words to me. I was far too young to consider how my destiny would unfold, but those words became permanently etched in my mind. Seven years later, my high school English teacher, Sue, gifted me with a journal book inscribed with the words: "never stop writing." Over the course of the subsequent years, I've been approached by prophets and laypeople who have all said the same thing; that I would one day write a book. Ironically, I have never had a desire to write a book, perhaps intimidated by the amount of time and effort it would require. But as the years passed, I could not escape the draw to write, whether it was poetry, song lyrics or journalizing, writing became my favorite pastime, the thing I consistently turned to whenever I wanted a creative release.

Twelve years ago, after undergoing major life changes, I found myself alone with God for the very first time. Thrust into a season of solitude, I came face-to-face with the presence of God, while engaging in the act of worship. The experiences I had worshiping God, unbeknownst to me, would become the framework for this book.

Reluctant to embrace my prophetic destiny, I soon began leading worship services and was presented with numerous opportunities to teach on the subject. In preparation for a worship workshop that I was to facilitate, I created an outline to distribute to the workshop attendees. With organized thoughts in tow, I pulled together all of my notes, strategically laid out my teaching in an easy to read format, and headed to Staples to have them color copied.

The event went off without a hitch, and I came home feeling completely accomplished. I felt that I had done the will of God for my life, and I could now relax and enjoy the memory of my one moment in the sun. Little did I know, the voice of God was about to ignite my destiny. While lying on the bed, I distinctly heard the Lord say: "I've given you the outline for your book; it's time to write it."

The last thing I ever intended to do was to write a book, and yet, here I am, having penned my first literary venture. I give all the glory to God because it is His grace that enabled me to do what I thought I could not do. This book is more than just sheets of paper bound together between two covers; it is the fulfillment of prophecy. It is a representation of God's power to accomplish His will in our lives in spite of any obstacles we face, or despite any limitations that we may set for ourselves. God is faithful to His word!

During this project, I had an uncanny experience which I believe confirms the message of this book. Whenever I traveled away from home, as customary for me to do, I visited different churches. For seven years, every church that I visited ironically featured a speaker who delivered a sermon on worship. Whether near or far, within the U.S. borders and abroad, across denominational lines and diverse cultural groups, in small venues and thousand seat arenas, the message was the same; "now is the time to worship." This made me understand that there is a global move currently underway awakening the Body of Christ to the significance that worship plays in our relationship with God. My voice is just one of many, in the sea of voices, proclaiming the same message; now is the time to worship God.

Finally, I'd be remiss if I did not tell you what you can and cannot expect from this book. This book is not an exhaustive theological dissertation about the topic of worship, but rather, it is an exhortation written to inspire people to engage in the act of worship. There are many books in print that delve into and dissect the topic of worship, and those books are needed and serve a valid purpose. However, I believe that we spend far more time talking about worship than we actually do engaging in worship. Knowledge about worship is great, but the application of that knowledge is even better. It's time for us to move collectively into the experiential realm of worship, the place where we put it into practice and spend quality time ministering to God. "But the time is coming and is already here, when by the power of God's Spirit people will worship the Father as he really is, offering him the true worship that he wants." –John 4:23 TEV

I

Worship is a beautiful spiritual
exchange that allows us to experience
God in the most significant way.

The Call to Worship

"Come, let us sing to the Lord! Let us give a joyous shout to the rock of our salvation! Let us come before him with thanksgiving. Let us sing him psalms of praise. For the Lord is a great God, the great King above all gods…Come, let us worship and bow down. Let us kneel before the Lord our maker, for he is our God. We are the people he watches over, the sheep under his care…" -Psalms 95:1-7

Sitting in the congregation of a local Church, I listened intently as the pastor delivered his sermon. Immediately following the service, the pastor posed an unexpected question to the audience: "How many of you have a passion for worshiping God and a desire to join the choir but are not gifted singers?" Many people raised their hands to acknowledge that they had this desire. As the pastor continued to address the church, he said God had given him a vision for a different kind of choir—one that consists of passionate worshipers rather than only talented singers. He said this move will change the focus of the choir; instead of concentrating solely on good singing, the focal point will be on pursuing the heart of God through passionate worship. He declared that within this renewed atmosphere of worship, a revival will take place that will unleash the Glory of God at a magnitude never seen before.

I imagine that scenarios like this are occurring all throughout the Body of Christ. Of course, not every choir director has revamped their worship team, but in one form or another, worship is being emphasized like never before. Even a casual observer can attest to this.

There is a worship movement sweeping through Christendom and it is causing a shift in church culture. Believers everywhere are starting to hunger for greater depth and intimacy with God. This desire for *more* of God is challenging church norms and revealing an overall dissatisfaction with the status quo. Our spiritual appetites are evolving and we're no longer content with practicing a religious model that does not include relationship-building with God.

The proof of this movement's existence is evidenced by the emergence of worship gatherings. Worship gatherings are springing up all over the nation—places where people are gathering together just to worship and seek God. Some of these meetings are hosted by well-known worship leaders, and others are spearheaded by unfamed men and women of God. Believers from all types of backgrounds and denominations are flocking to these meetings just to be in a space where they can express their worship and connect directly with God.

The momentum of these gatherings is spilling over into our church services, prompting extended times of worship that suspend business as usual.

Something is happening! Perhaps no one voice can fully articulate the depth of what's brewing, but something big is coming to the church.

As we stand on the precipice of this great shift, worship is at the forefront in this hour for one purpose: to lead us into an encounter with God. In the place of worship, God makes His presence known to us, draws us near to Himself and fills us with His love. This is the experience that our hearts are longing for.

God's Love Language

In his book *The Five Love Languages*, best-selling author Dr. Gary Chapman presents a concept called "love language." Written primarily for married couples, the book theorizes that in relationships we all speak a primary love language which falls into one of five categories; quality time, words of affirmation, acts of service, physical touch, and receiving gifts. Essentially, each person has a primary love language through which they prefer to receive love, and to successfully communicate love; it needs to be expressed in the language of the person to whom we are giving it to. When love is expressed in the language that we speak, Dr. Chapman asserts, our "love tank" is full and we feel emotionally loved and secure.

After reading this book, I couldn't help but wonder whether this concept could also be applied to my relationship with God. If so, the obvious questions would be the following: What is God's primary love language? And is it possible for me to express my love for Him in a way that touches Him like nothing else can? The answer to the latter question is yes. The Bible presents overwhelming evidence that God loves worship. He loves it so much that He chose to surround Himself with it for all eternity, (Revelation 4:8). Surely, something so valued and desired by God leaves no room for mystery and points us directly to the answer. In the context of this concept, I believe God's primary love language is worship. When we worship God, it fills Him up and captures His heart. It's the one thing we can do that touches Him like nothing else can.

The idea that we can affect God's heart is a remarkable

thought to reflect on. It may even seem too good to be true that a God who is all-knowing, all-powerful, all-loving, and who has no need of anything, is moved by our acts of worship to Him. But, when we consider that there are over 172 biblical references to the subject of worship, it becomes undeniably clear that God has placed a high premium on it.

Let's analyze the implications of one of the most extravagant acts of worship recorded in the Bible. The book of Luke details an incident of a woman who washed Jesus' feet. The event presumably took place in Galilee, against a backdrop of a dinner party. As the story unfolds, Jesus is at the home of Simon the Pharisee, a member of the religious elite. When a certain unnamed woman heard that Jesus was there, she went to Simon's house and brought an alabaster jar filled with expensive perfume. Upon seeing Jesus, the woman knelt at His feet and started to cry. As she wept, her tears fell on his feet and she wiped them off with her hair. Then, she kissed His feet and poured the entire jar of perfume on them.

When Simon witnessed the scene between Jesus and the woman, he inwardly disapproved of the woman's actions. Being a self-righteous elitist, Simon looked down on the woman because she was a known sinner. He felt that Jesus should have perceived how unworthy she was and not have allowed her to anoint His feet. Jesus discerned Simon's thoughts and promptly rebuked him, and then praised the unnamed woman for her deeds, (see Luke 7:36-50).

Luke's narrative does not reveal what motivated this woman's actions, so at this point, we're left to speculate about what led her to this moment. Perhaps Jesus did something wonderful for her and she came to thank Him, or maybe she was seeking forgiveness for her sins. Whatever the reason was, the magnitude of her actions spoke volumes.

This woman went to great lengths to anoint Jesus' feet; she

withstood harsh criticism and acquired very costly perfume. The fragrance that was used to anoint Jesus' feet would have cost about a year's worth of wages — the amount of money that a working person would earn in an entire year. Imagine spending your annual income on a bottle of perfume. Now, imagine pouring all of it on someone's feet. That is the equivalent of what the unnamed woman did.

The unnamed woman was not a wealthy person so the perfume very likely represented her entire life's savings; it is also likely that she purchased the perfume specifically for this occasion. Such an extravagant act of sacrifice had a profound impact on Jesus.

In response to this woman's act of worship, Jesus made the following statement to Simon:

> *"You neglected the courtesy of olive oil to anoint my head, but she has anointed my feet with rare perfume. I tell you, her sins--and they are many--have been forgiven, so she has shown me much love." -Luke 7:46-47 NLT*

This is the only example in the Bible where Jesus says that someone demonstrated love to Him. In other words, the only time in the entire Bible when Jesus felt love was when He was being worshiped. What a stunning revelation!

I believe Jesus' statement does the following three things: 1) defines the role of worship; 2) establishes the relevancy of worship; 3) supports the concept that worship is God's love language.

If worship is the primary language through which God receives love, then that makes it an invaluable practice in our quest to know Him more. Not only is worship a means for us to commune with God, it's also a means for Him to commune with us. As we pour out our love on Him, He in turn pours out His love on us.   It's a beautiful spiritual exchange that allows us to experience God in the most significant way.

What is Worship?

Worship is defined as the act of reverence rendered to a deity to demonstrate love and admiration. It is a voluntary act of our will to express devotion, commitment and complete surrender to God. Worship also means to make oneself low, signifying that humility is the proper posture of worship—the acknowledgment of your absolute dependence on God as the source of your life. There are different acts and expressions of worship, but the shared characteristic which links them all is that every act or expression of worship is done solely to honor God.   True   worship is God-centered worship; where He alone is the object of affection. Nothing higher than God exists, and there is no one else like Him; He is sovereign, He is our maker, and we owe Him our worship.

Within each of us, there is a natural inclination to worship, but if this desire isn't directed toward God, we will inevitably worship something or someone else to satisfy that longing in our soul. There is evidence of this all over the world; in every culture, there is something or someone to whom people pay homage to. There are even those who don't express their worship in traditional ways; rather, they worship their possessions, their achievements, their careers, their families, and so on. Regardless of what the object of focus is, it is apparent that people cannot resist the draw to worship something. God put this desire within each of us so that we would naturally be drawn to worship Him, as we were created for His pleasure (see Revelation 4:11).   God derives immense pleasure from our worship (to Him), but He is saddened when we replace Him with other things toward which we direct our worship. God should hold first place in our lives, and our worship should be reserved exclusively for Him. We should never worship idols or false gods or exalt anything above the one true living God (see Exodus 20:4–5).

Why Worship

✞ We worship God because we love Him, and we love Him because He first loved us. We are commanded to *"...love the Lord thy God with all thy heart, and with all thy soul, and with all thy mind, and with all thy strength..."* (Mark 12:30). The primary reason we worship God is because we love Him, and worshiping God is the most profound thing we can do to demonstrate our love for Him.

✞ We worship God because He desires it; God is actually looking for people who will worship Him (see John 4:23). The fact that God is "looking" implies that He is actively searching for something that He sincerely wants. If someone you love had a desire that was within your ability to fulfill, you'd go the distance to effectuate their wish just for a chance to show how much you love them. In the same manner, our heavenly Father has a desire that is within our ability to fulfill; He desires worship. Hence, as an act of love, we should willingly give God what He wants, which is our worship.

✞ We worship God because He deserves it; *"Give unto the Lord the glory due unto his name; worship the Lord in the beauty of holiness"* (Psalms 29:2). Consider all of the grand monuments that have been erected to honor the lives of notable historical figures. To deserve such memorials, these esteemed individuals had to accomplish something exceptional that benefited either their country or the world at large. If we attempted to quantify the value of all their contributions, the total would be minuscule in comparison to what God did for humanity. God's act of redemption, through the shed blood of Jesus Christ, trumps every contribution – past, present, and future – that anyone can make. So when you think of honor, God is worthy of it all. Worship is due to Him for all that He has done for us.

✞   We worship God because everyone is called to worship Him; *"All the ends of the world shall remember and turn unto the Lord: and all the kindred's of the nations shall worship before thee"* (Psalms 22:27). Worship is a global affair. Every man, woman and child, of every race, creed and nationality, in every part of the world is called to worship God. Human history will culminate in worship (Isaiah 45:22-23).

Worship and Singing

"All the earth shall worship thee, and shall sing unto thee; they shall sing to thy name." -Psalms 66:4

Singing is a central component of worship. While there are various expressions of worship, the Bible shows that God has placed an enormous value on song. When the apostle John was exiled to the Island of Patmos, he had a supernatural visitation that he records in the book of Revelation. John was in the spirit, and he looked up and saw a door standing open in heaven. He was taken up and allowed to witness the realm of worship that surrounds the throne of God. What he observed reveals to us how significant singing is to God:

*"Then I looked again, and I heard the **singing** of thousands and millions of angels around the throne…and they **sang** in a mighty chorus…"* -Revelation 5:11-12

This verse paints a picture of God's dwelling place; He is enthroned in worship, surrounded by an innumerable company of angels that sing to Him continuously. God is infinite, and He has chosen to surround Himself with infinite singing, this fact alone should indicate how important song is to God. Singing to the Lord is the most intimate form of worship that we can offer Him. Imagine a marriage relationship, one of the most passionate acts a spouse can perform to affirm their love for their mate would be to sing them a love song. Nothing could be more pleasing and endearing than to be the recipient of such a heartfelt gesture. This is how our singing touches God; it melts His heart.

"...come before his presence with singing." -Psalms 100:2

It is virtually impossible to negate the importance of worshiping God through song. The Bible contains over four hundred references to singing and fifty direct commands to sing.

Singing is an innate instinct; it is a part of the human nature. Everyone has an urge and a readiness to sing without any hesitation; this is why we make melody over most things that we do.[1] We sing in the shower, while performing household tasks, driving in the car, when cradling a child, the list goes on and on. There is a song on the inside of us all; God designed it to be so.

Singing is universal; there is no culture, regardless of how remote or isolated, that does not sing. Singing has been an important part of human behavior all throughout history. Our ancient ancestors began to sing soon after developing vocal chords, and before they could actually speak.

Research even shows that singing is good for your physical and psychological health. It alleviates anxiety, lowers stress levels, promotes a healthy heart, and enhances ones mental state.[2] While these benefits may be surprising, they lead us to an exciting conclusion: singing is fundamentally enriching.

Almost everyone can admit to singing out loud unashamedly when they are alone, but many of those same people also have a fear of singing in the presence of others, or when one-on-one with God. Although singing is a very natural thing to do, the freedom to sing is sometimes stifled in us for different

---

[1] www.desiringgod.org, Why Is Singing So Important for Christians?
[2] www.businessballs.com, Singing, © Sally Garozzo and Alan Chapman 2011.

reasons. Perhaps we've been told negative messages about our singing ability, or maybe we compared our voice with someone else's and felt that ours didn't measure up. Whatever the reason may be, the result is that singing out loud invokes feelings of discomfort in many of us. In spite of our discomfort, however, we must endeavor to overcome our inhibitions so that we can worship God in a way that truly pleases Him.

When it comes to worship, your singing ability does not matter to God nor can lack of skill disqualify you from worshiping Him. Your vocal capabilities are unimportant to God because He created your voice; your sound is beautiful to Him even if you're not considered a 'gifted' singer. What is important to God is the origin of your worship, where it is coming from. True worship flows from the inside out. It originates in your heart and expresses itself outwardly through an "act" of worship. Singing is an *act* of worship, but if it has no inward affection as its basis, God is not pleased with your song. Worship that pleases God is one that is heartfelt and pure. If the origin of your worship is sincere, then God is delighted with your singing, even if you lack musical abilities.

Unfortunately, some Christians have an incorrect view about singing to God; they believe that it's either unnecessary or insignificant, and they don't see the value in it. There are also some who are so uncomfortable with singing that they ignore it all together. These dispositions are problematic because God designed singing to be a way for us to engage His presence. If we ignore song, we go against a divinely inspired pathway that leads to the manifested presence of God. As Christians, if we never experience God's manifested presence, how can we ever truly know him?

God's Manifested Presence

There are three dimensions of God's presence, and it's

helpful for us to know them so as to eliminate any confusion surrounding the topic of the manifested presence of God. First, there is His omnipresence. This means that God is present everywhere, at all times, whether we realize it or not, (Jeremiah 23:23-24; Psalms 139:7-10). Second, there is the indwelling presence of God. God's presence dwells on the inside of every Christian by the power of His Holy Spirit, (I Corinthians 3:16, John 15:4-5). The third dimension of God's presence is what we refer to as His manifested presence. In the Old Testament, this dimension of God's presence was often called the Shekinah Glory. It's when God reveals Himself in a living, present, almost tangible way, in particular times and places. This is the facet of God's presence that Moses encountered at the burning bush, (Exodus 3), and it's the facet that David was referring to when he said, "Cast me not away from thy presence..." (Psalms 51:11). It's called the manifest presence because it comes with manifestations of God's person, whether it is His goodness, love, peace, or the demonstration of His power through the operation of the gifts of the spirit (I Corinthians 12:1-11), there is always a marked distinction when the manifested presence of God is at hand. Biblically, we can create conditions that attract the manifested presence of God; such as worshiping Him and honoring Him with the fruit of our lips, (Psalms 22:3). When we worship God and hunger for Him, He responds by revealing Himself to us in a real and present way. This is the manifest presence of God.

The general Hebrew term for "presence" is panim, which translated means "face," implying a close and personal encounter with the Lord.[1] Worship brings you face-to-face with the presence of God and allows you to encounter Him in a very personal way. This dynamic experience is available to all Believers who choose to sing and glorify God with the fruit of their lips.

---

[1] www.biblestudytools.com, Presence of God, by Bryan E. Beyer

Sincerity vs. Tradition

Worship is key to experiencing God's presence, but it's important to understand that God does not respond to worship that is merely offered as an act of tradition. God responds to sincerity, and His presence is released in direct proportion to our heart's passion and desire for Him. If we attempt to worship God out of tradition or a false sense of obligation, we will miss the blessing of worship. The purpose of worship is to experience God in a real and meaningful way, but we can only do that if our hearts are engaged.

I grew up in a church where the worship service was purely based on religious tradition; we sang church hymns *about* God but not directed *to* God. As a result, my worship was disingenuous and mechanical, in fact, most of the time that I was singing 'about God' I wasn't even thinking about God. Looking back to those earlier days, I now realize that I never once had a genuine worship experience with God because my heart was not in it. The same is true for many of us today.

The problem with tradition and obligation is that tradition can reduce the sacredness of worship into a monotonous routine activity, and things done out of obligation are oftentimes burdensome and insincere. God wants sincerity, and sincerity comes from your heart, whereas, tradition and obligation are erroneous mindsets that stem from your intellect (your head). Many devout Christians have yet to transition from head to heart worship, but that is the paradigm shift that Jesus taught when He ministered to the woman at the well:

> *"The woman saith unto him, Sir, I perceive that thou art a prophet. Our fathers worshiped in this mountain; and ye say, that in Jerusalem is the place where men ought to worship. Jesus saith unto her, Woman, believe me, the hour cometh, when ye shall neither in this mountain, nor*

yet at Jerusalem, worship the Father. Ye worship ye know not what: we know what we worship: for salvation is of the Jews. But the hour cometh, and now is when the true worshippers shall worship the Father in spirit and in truth: for the Father seeketh such to worship him. God is a Spirit: and they that worship him must worship him in spirit and in truth." -John 4:21-24

The woman at the well identified worship with tradition, and she had no intimate knowledge of the God that she worshiped. She was going to a place, participating in religious customs, which her forefathers practiced and handed down to her. Jesus was showing her the new place of worship; that instead of a geographical location, worship would take place spirit to spirit, heart to heart.

Today, worship is no longer an impersonal act centered on traditionalism; it is an engaging communion with the Spirit of God. Therefore, we should not approach it with an insipid attitude void of emotion; we should worship God with passion and vibrancy, and come before Him fully expecting to encounter His glory.

The Acceptable Sacrifice

"...let us offer the sacrifice of praise to God continually, that is, the fruit of our lips..." -Hebrews 13:15

When worship is expressed to God it is an offering, and anything that is presented as an offering can either be accepted or rejected depending on its quality. In the Old Testament era, animal sacrifices were a common part of religious worship. A person would bring an animal to the altar of God, and the Priests would burn it and the smoke from the sacrifice ascended to the heavens as "a soothing aroma to the Lord" (Leviticus 1:9). This practice was instituted to provide a temporary covering of sins and to foreshadow the perfect and complete sacrifice of Jesus Christ

(Leviticus 4:35, 5:10).   When Jesus died on the cross, all animal sacrifices came to an end and a new system of worship was established.   Instead of bringing animals to God, we are now commanded to bring spiritual sacrifices to Him (Hebrews 9:23; I Peter 2:5).   The "fruit of our lips" is a spiritual sacrifice which we now present to God as a worship offering.

While the old system is no longer in place, it featured a quality requirement that is conceptually still applicable in our modern-day worship.   At the time when animal sacrifices were acceptable, you couldn't just bring any animal to God; you were required to bring the best of the best—an animal without any ailments, spots or blemishes.   If there were any defects found in your animal, it was considered unacceptable and detestable to God.

As New Testament worshipers, we should bring acceptable sacrifices to God—the best of what we have to give. We shouldn't take worship lightly and assume that He will accept whatever we offer.   Just as there was a set standard for animal sacrifices, there is also a set standard for our spiritual sacrifices.   If we want our worship to be acceptable to the Lord, we must give Him our whole heart.   This is the quality standard which determines whether or not God receives our worship.

"...I will praise the Lord with my whole heart..."
-Psalms 111:1

You "heart" is the vital center and source of your being, emotions, sensibilities, personality and attributes.   It's the repository of your deepest and sincerest feelings and beliefs, (as defined by Webster's Dictionary).   In effect, this verse is saying: I will praise the Lord from the deepest center of my being, with all of my senses, emotions and sincerest feelings.   This is the acceptable sacrifice of worship!

When your worship meets God's standards, that is, when you worship Him with your whole heart, the heavens open and He comes down to dwell in your midst. Insincere worship, on the other hand, one which merely *portrays* a form of depth and sincerity, has no capacity to reach heaven and is a missed opportunity for a God encounter. Cain discovered this when he presumptuously offered an unacceptable sacrifice to God:

> *"And in process of time it came to pass that Cain brought of the fruit of the ground an offering unto the Lord. And Abel, he also brought of the firstlings of his flock and of the fat thereof. And the Lord had respect unto Abel and to his offering: But unto Cain and to his offering he had no respect. And Cain was very wroth and his countenance fell. And the Lord said unto Cain, Why art thou wroth? And why is thy countenance fallen? If thou doest well, shalt thou not be accepted?" –Genesis 4:3-7*

Cain assumed that God would accept whatever he offered, just as long as he brought Him an offering, but he was terribly wrong. God rejected Cain's offering because it did not meet His conditions. Instead of giving God what He required, Cain gave God what was convenient for him to give and then became angry with God because God would not acquiesce. Cain did things on his own terms and had no regard for God. He had an opportunity to honor the Lord, but he took it lightly and inevitably missed out on a blessing.

In today's environment, many of us make the same mistake; we assume that God will accept *whatever* we offer Him, just as long as we *perform* the act of worship. But similar to Cain, that is wrong. Worship should never be done out of pretense, with an insincere motive or out of a false sense of obligation. Worship should be done with a willing heart and an attitude of reverence, humility, and submission to God.

What God Wants

"The LORD looks down from heaven on the entire human race; he looks to see if there is even one with real understanding, one who seeks for God." -Psalms 14:2 NLT

More than anything, God wants to be pursued; He wants us to desire Him with the same longing that He has for us.

God has always desired a close relationship with His children; this has been His plan from the very beginning. Before Adam sinned in the Garden of Eden (Genesis chapter 3), both he and Eve knew God on an intimate, personal level. They walked with Him, they talked with Him, and they had unlimited access to His presence. This is the type of relationship that God intended to have with all of His children. But as a result of Adam and Eve's sin, man became separated and disconnected from God. This fallout from sin, however, did not change God's original plan to have a close connection with man. In fact, from the point of the fall until now, God has been trying to get us back to the intimate relationship that He shared with Adam and Eve in the Garden.

In response to God's desire for a close connection with us, He wants us to seek after Him and make an effort to build a relationship with Him. He wants to be the center of our lives and have ongoing communion with us just like He did with Adam and Eve.

When we take the time to worship, we demonstrate to God that we want to be with Him and that we want to know Him in a greater way. Moreover, worship is a foundational part of relationship-building with God, and when we engage in it, we're able to experience Him the way He originally intended.

The worshiper who chooses to seek after God will encounter infinite dimensions of His glory and have perpetual access to His inner courts. They will delight in His presence and experience a passion for Him that is unsurpassed by all of their carnal desires.

Who We Worship

God cannot entirely be defined within the confines of language, so every attempt to describe Him is incomplete. The Bible, however, does paint an incredible picture of God's nature and His capabilities, thereby giving us a frame of reference to be able to identify how He operates. The challenge many of us face is that we've become so familiar with the theology of God that we either take the Bible for granted or, we read it as if it's fictional. We forget that the Bible is divinely inspired, historical documentation of actual events that occurred before we got here. So then, we must be cautious not to allow our minds to reduce God to someone who's on our level, because He's not. He's a supernatural, self-sustaining, sovereign, omnipotent, awesome wonder, and He thrives on worship. Furthermore, that is why worship is so powerful, because it creates an environment for God to move in, and when God moves, He moves according to His nature and His ability. So who is this God that we worship?

✞   God is the ***creator***, nothing and no one exists higher than God (Isaiah 40:28). He is the one who caused everything to come into existence. "In the beginning God created the heavens and the earth. The earth was an empty, formless mass cloaked in darkness" (Genesis 1:1-2), then God spoke, and whatever He said came into existence. "...the entire universe was formed at God's command, (and) what we now see did not come from anything that can be seen" (Hebrews 11:3). Nothing existed before God created it, and He did not use anything to bring into existence what He created.

The miracle of Jesus' birth attests to the creative nature of

God. For Jesus to have the power to destroy sin's control over mankind, it was necessary for Him to be deity and humanity at the same time.   Naturally this was an impossible feat because it defies the laws that govern human anatomy; but God is not subject to -or limited by- anything outside of Himself.   In one of the greatest phenomenon's that has ever occurred, God ***created*** an embryo inside of Mary's uterus without the use of male sperm (Luke 1:26-37).   What a grand display of the creative power of our God;   He is the only entity that exists who can create without the use of a creating agent. This is **who** we worship!

✟   God is ***Almighty***, "we cannot imagine the power of the Almighty…" (Job 37:23). The word Almighty means: all powerful. Our God has all vigor, force, strength, ability and legal authority to do or act. When God acts, the force of His power cannot be stopped.

God's power was extraordinarily demonstrated on behalf of the Israelites on numerous occasions and at various junctures. The emancipation of the Israelites was a pivotal time in biblical history because had it not been for the power of God, the Israelites would have remained under enemy control. But God delivered them, and the methods He used illustrate to us that His power is supreme, matchless and unrivaled.   During the Israelites historic pilgrimage from Egypt to Canaan, the Lord led them by way of the wilderness. At the same time, their former taskmaster began to regret setting them free (Exodus 14:5), so Pharaoh assembled together all of his troops and set out to pursue the Israelites, expecting to recapture them.

Not long after, the Egyptians caught up with the Israelites as they were camped along the shore of the Red Sea. When the Israelites saw Pharaoh and his army approaching, they started to panic; almost immediately they turned against

Moses (their deliverer) and complained about ever being delivered in the first place. But Moses began to encourage them in the Lord, and he prophesied that "the Egyptians you see today will never be seen again, the Lord himself will fight for you" (Exodus 14:13-14). Then the Lord commanded Moses to raise his shepherd's staff over the sea, "and the Lord opened up a path through the water with a <u>strong east wind</u>... turning the sea into dry land." (Exodus 13:21-22) This was not a manmade lake with no undercurrent, nor was this a river streaming along a brook next to green pastures. This was a massive ocean and the "strong east wind" that parted the Red Sea was the force of the power of the *Almighty* God. This is <u>**who**</u> we worship!

As part of God's covenant promise to Israel, He gave them the land of Canaan as an inheritance, but when the time came for the Israelites to inhabit their land, it was occupied by the Canaanites, a cursed people. To receive what God had promised, they would have to fight for the land, one city at a time. The first city to be conquered was Jericho, a city fortified by walls and gates. "Now the gates of Jericho were tightly shut because the people were afraid of the Israelites. No one was allowed to go in or out" (Joshua 6:1). The Lord instructed Joshua to have his entire army (this included 7 priests and the Ark of the Covenant, which was the presence of God), march around the city once a day for 6 days, and on the 7th day, march around the city 7 times. On the 7th day, the walls of Jericho collapsed! The Israelites did not use dynamite, a battering ram, a bulldozer, a wrecking ball, or any of the other tools that a modern day 21st century construction crew would have needed to bring down those walls. It was the sheer force of the power of the *Almighty* God that brought down the walls of Jericho. This is <u>**who**</u> we worship!

✟   God is a ***fortress***. "The Lord is my rock, and my fortress, and my deliverer; my God, my strength, in whom I will trust; my buckler, and the horn of my salvation, and my high tower" (Psalms 18:2).   As a fortress, the Lord strengthens you against attacks; He builds you up so that you're secure and fortified.   He deliverers you, liberates you and rescues you. He is a buckler–the perfect shield that wards off every blow. This is <u>***who***</u> we worship!

✟   God is a ***shepherd***.   "He shall feed his flock like a shepherd: he shall gather the lambs with his arm, and carry them in his bosom, and shall gently lead those that are with young" (Isaiah 40:11). Like a shepherd, God will watch over you and make sure that you have everything you need. He will lead and guide you in peaceful paths, out of harm's way. He repairs the broken areas of your heart. He will honor you and bestow blessings upon you right in front of your enemies, and He will cause His goodness and mercy to pursue you so that your cup overflows with blessings (Psalms 23).

After Elijah prophesied to King Ahab that there would be a drought for the next 3 years, the Lord sent Elijah into hiding. "Go to the east and hide by Kerith Brook..., drink from the brook and eat what the ravens bring you, for I have commanded them to bring you food" (I Kings 17:2-4). As a result of the drought, the brook eventually dried up, so the Lord sent Elijah to live in the village of Zarephath and He told him, "There is a widow there who will feed you. I have given her my instructions" (I Kings 17:8). Elijah was led and cared for by the great ***shepherd***; God supernaturally watched over him and made sure that he had everything he needed to survive the drought. This is <u>***who***</u> we worship!

✟   God is a ***healer***. "...for I am the Lord who heals you" (Exodus 15:26). God can cure any disease, mend wounds, restore health, and make (you) well again.   God healed

Rebekah from infertility (without the use of medical science), and she conceived twins (Genesis 25:21). God healed Naaman from leprosy (an incurable skin disease characterized by ulcers, white scaly scabs and deformities), and his skin became as soft as a young child's skin (II Kings 5:14-15). God healed Hezekiah from a terminal illness and added 15 more years to his life, (II Kings 20:1-6). This is *who* we worship!

✚ God is a God of *covenant*. "Know therefore that the Lord thy God, he is God, the faithful God, which keepeth covenant and mercy with them that love him and keep his commandments to a thousand generations" (Deuteronomy 7:9). A covenant is a promise, and when God makes a promise it's guaranteed to come to pass. God has established 8 covenants with us (Believers) and these covenants illustrate what God desires for us: The Edenic Covenant (Genesis 1:28), The Adamic Covenant (Genesis 3:15), The Noahic Covenant (Genesis 8:21, 9:8-17), The Abrahamic Covenant (Genesis 12:2-3, 17:1-7, 22:15-18), The Mosaic Covenant (Exodus 19:3-6, Rev. 1:6), The Palestinian Covenant (Leviticus 26:4-13, Deuteronomy 28:1-13), The Davidic Covenant (II Samuel 7:12-13, 16, I Chronicles 17:11-14), and The New Covenant (Hebrews 8:7-13, Hebrews 9 &10, Hebrews 10:16-18). These covenant promises include: redemption, eternal life, protection, preservation, blessings, the faithfulness of God, etc. We can fully be assured that God will fulfill His promises in our lives because He keeps covenant to a thousand generations. This is *who* we worship!

✚ God is a *merciful* and *forgiving* God. "The Lord is merciful and gracious, slow to anger, and plenteous in mercy. He will not always reprimand, neither will he keep his anger forever. He has not dealt with us after our sins, nor rewarded us according to our iniquities. For as the heaven is high above the earth, so great is his mercy toward them that fear him. As far as the east is from the west, so far has he removed our transgressions from us" (Psalms 103:8-12). God is compassionate and kind without measure. It's His disposition; He would rather forgive than punish. This is **_who_** we worship!

The God we worship is the same yesterday, today and forever, and when we worship Him, we create an environment for Him to move in. When God moves, He moves according to His nature and His ability. This makes the atmosphere of worship a spiritual arena filled with power and unending possibilities. There are no limits to what can happen in the atmosphere of worship; miracles can occur in worship, battles can be won in worship, healing can manifest in worship, the prophetic voice can speak in worship, restoration can flow in worship, blessings can be released in worship, strength can be renewed in worship, and deliverance can come through worship. Anything can happen when we begin to worship God, because God dwells in the atmosphere of worship (see Psalms 22:3).

Summary

Worship is the primary language through which God prefers to receive love. When we worship God, it fills Him up and captures His heart like nothing else can. God desires all of His children to worship Him and to actively seek His face. He has given each of us an invitation to come into His presence, and now He is looking for a response... He is looking for worshipers.

Action Point:

1. Respond to His invitation by committing to set aside 30 minutes (or more) each day for worship.

    If you're unsure how to begin, start with your favorite worship CD and sing to God. If singing is uncomfortable for you, stick with it until you overcome the discomfort of it. Eventually, you'll begin singing to God with ease and you'll enjoy worshiping Him in song.

Pray this prayer:

    Dear Heavenly Father, I thank you for inviting me to worship you. I believe that you are looking for worshipers and I want to be found by you. Transform me into a true worshiper. Please give me a hunger and a desire for your presence, and unlock my emotions so that I can be intimate with you. Ignite passion within me and cause me to thirst for you. Help me to identify and eliminate every distraction that attempts to hinder my commitment to pursuing you consistently. Thank you for giving me the privilege of worshiping you, you are a loving Father and I honor you, in Jesus' name, Amen.

II

---

*The condition of your heart determines
the value of your worship.*

The Heart of a Worshiper

"Who shall ascend into the hill of the Lord? Or who shall stand in his holy place.
He that hath clean hands, and a pure heart..." -Psalms 24:3-4

*Y*our worship is the fragrance of your heart. If your heart is pure, your worship produces a sweet smelling savor that is very pleasing to God. The other side of that is; an impure heart reduces the potency of your worship, making it unappealing and uninviting to God. There is a unique connection between your heart and your worship and if you desire to be the type of worshiper that God is seeking, you must examine the spiritual health of your heart. Having a spiritually healthy heart is as important to your worship life as a physically healthy heart is to your natural life.

> *"Who shall ascend into the hill of the Lord? Or who shall stand in his holy place." -Psalms 24:3*

The writer of this Psalm asks a rhetorical question to highlight the fact that there is a prerequisite for entering the presence of God; the requirement is that you must have a pure heart. An unclean heart will limit your access to the presence of God and negatively affect the quality of your worship. Worship begins in your heart, so it is extremely vital to cultivate and maintain a clean heart so that your worship is not compromised. The condition of your heart is not fully known to you, only God has the ability to see the true state of your heart. You can actually be deceived and misled by your own heart because it has the capacity to contain evil (Jeremiah 17:10). For this reason, it is important that you ask God to purify your heart from all unrighteousness.

> *"Create in me a clean heart, O God; and renew a right spirit within me." -Psalms 51:10*

The condition of your heart determines the *value* of your worship. In worship, you can sing like the most beautiful singer in the world, you can bow down before God, lay prostrate at the altar, or have hands lifted with tears flowing down your face, but if your heart is not right, your worship amounts to very little. There are many acts of worship, but the question is; "what's going on in your heart?" God looks on the heart (I Samuel 16:7).

> *"Blessed are the pure in heart for they shall see God."*
> *—Matthew 5:8*

The Webster's New World Dictionary defines *pure* as: free from anything that adulterates, contaminates, taints, spoils or, pollutes. Using the dictionary's definition of *pure*, the real meaning of what Jesus said is: blessed are those that are free from anything that adulterates, contaminates, taints, spoils or, pollutes their heart, for they shall see God.

Pollutants come in many forms, oftentimes they are obvious and easy to detect, but sometimes they go unnoticed and slither their way right into the heart. Sin and disobedience are obvious heart pollutants, but there are also attitudes and behaviors that can pollute the heart as well.   So when we consider the condition of our hearts relative to our worship, it is crucial that we fully understand the standard of purity that God has established for the heart.

Issues of the Heart

✝   *"If I regard iniquity in my heart, the Lord will not hear me."* (Psalms 66:18) *"For from within, [that is] out of the heart of men, come base and wicked thoughts, sexual immorality, stealing, murder, adultery, coveting (a greedy desire to have more wealth), dangerous and destructive wickedness, deceit, unrestrained (indecent) conduct; an evil eye (envy), slander (evil speaking, malicious misrepresentation, abusiveness), pride (the sin of an uplifted heart against God and man), foolishness (folly, lack of sense, recklessness, thoughtlessness). All these evil [purposes and desires] come from within, and they make the man unclean and render him unhallowed."* (Mark 7:21-23 AMP)   It is an abomination to offer worship to God while actively practicing sin (Isaiah 1:11-18). Before you approach the presence of God, if your heart is defiled with iniquity, you must acknowledge your transgression(s) and repent.   Worship does not hide sin!   God is holy, righteous and pure, and sin cannot come into His presence. The Bible gives us an illustrative example of this in the Old Testament during the time of the Levitical priesthood. According to scripture, in those days, only Priests were allowed into the presence of God (the holy of holies), but prior to entering His presence, they had to perform cleansing rites (that were customary at that time) to purify themselves from all sin.   If they failed to cleanse themselves before going into the holy of holies, immediately upon entering God's presence, they dropped dead!

If we want God to accept our worship, the primary

requirement is that we repent and turn from all known sin. "If we confess our sins, he is faithful and just to forgive us our sins, and to cleanse us from all unrighteousness." (1 John 1:9)

✟   *"Everyone that is proud in heart is an abomination to the Lord..." (Proverbs 16:5).*   Pride denotes having an excessively high opinion of oneself; referring to someone that is very haughty and/or arrogant. Pride is an insidious disposition into which it is very easy to fall, particularly because we live in a society where class-ism is a socially accepted form of prejudice. At any given time you can esteem yourself more highly than others simply based on your rank. It takes humility to place as much value on others as you do yourself.

God hates pride, and I believe one reason why it offends Him so much is because it dishonors Jesus' life. Mankind was doomed and destined for destruction until God – moved by unimaginable love and compassion – intervened. He sent His son Jesus to rescue us from a very dismal yet certain fate. When Jesus gave up His life in exchange for ours, He restored us back to right standing with God. Now, we are once again sons and daughters of God, and when God looks at us, He sees Jesus. That is why God is "no respecter of persons," (Acts 10:34), because Jesus leveled the playing field and made us all the same in Him. In God's eyes, we desecrate the cross of Christ when we regard ourselves above others, because neither of us would be worth anything if it weren't for Jesus. In Him, we equally hold the highest ranking position that exists: "heirs of the kingdom," and that is the pinnacle of positions that anyone could ever attain. Everything that we are, we are because of the sacrifice that Jesus made for us. So then, pride is a baseless, insolent, audacious attitude, which I believe is a stench in the nostrils of God.

According to heaven's history records, pride originated inside of Lucifer's heart. Lucifer was the "signet of perfection, full of wisdom and perfect in beauty." He lived on the "holy mountain of God" where he had the privilege to cover the throne of God with his worship. Lucifer enjoyed unlimited access to the presence of God until the day that "unrighteousness" was found in him. Due to his own magnificence, Lucifer's heart became lifted up in pride. He foolishly accredited himself for his own splendor, instead of acknowledging that it was bestowed upon him by God. This deviation from truth caused his heart to become lifted above God in pride, and he began to desire God's glory for himself. The end result is that Lucifer was cast down from the holy mountain and eternally banished from the presence of God (Ezekiel 28:1-18).

Now, from his fallen position, Satan attempts to hinder God's worship by ensnaring hearts in pride. It takes humility to worship God as the source of your life, but pride will prevent you from humbling yourself and acknowledging your need for Him. Pride can also keep you from being vulnerable with God because it makes you feel as if you have to maintain control over your emotions. Pride will even make you ashamed and embarrassed to worship God in front of others, for fear of what they may think of you. Ultimately, as seen in Lucifer's demise, pride will cause you to fall (Proverbs 16:18).

Such was the case with King Nebuchadnezzar. King Nebuchadnezzar was a great king who built a huge empire and had enormous influence in Babylon. One night in a dream God warned Nebuchadnezzar that pride was going to be his downfall. Unfortunately, the King failed to take heed to God's warning. Twelve months after that prophetic dream, King Nebuchadnezzar walked into his royal palace and as he looked out across the city, he said, "Is not this great Babylon that I have built for the house of the kingdom by the might of my power, and for the honor of my majesty?" While the words were yet in his mouth, a voice came down from heaven saying, "You are no longer ruler of this kingdom. You will be driven from human society. You will live in the fields with the wild animals, and you will eat grass like a cow. Seven years will pass while you live this way, until you learn that the Most High rules over the kingdoms of the world and gives them to anyone he chooses." After seven years passed, Nebuchadnezzar looked up to heaven and his sanity returned and he worshiped the Lord as the Most High God who lives forever and whose dominion is everlasting, and whose kingdom is eternal. (See Daniel 4)

King Nebuchadnezzar lost everything because he did not acknowledge God as the source of his success; as a result of pride, he took God's glory for himself. During those seven years that Nebuchadnezzar spent in insanity, God humbled him to the position of a worshiper, and when he offered praise to God, the Lord restored him back as the King over Babylon.

Pride and humility are polar opposites and they have two very different effects on your worship. A humble heart will draw God to you and create a dwelling place for His presence (Isaiah 57:15). In contrast, a prideful heart will cause God to reject your worship, because "God resists the proud, but gives grace to the humble" (James 4:6). Humility is the only posture of true God-centered worship.

✞ *"So likewise shall my heavenly Father do also unto you, if ye from your hearts forgive not every one his brother their trespasses."* (Matthew 18:35) In response to Peter's inquiry about the necessity of forgiveness, Jesus used an allegory to demonstrate to him how important it is to forgive. Jesus told a story of an unforgiving debtor who owed a King millions of dollars but couldn't repay him. The debtor pleaded for forgiveness of the debt and received it. While the debtor was leaving the King's house, he saw someone that owed him a few dollars. That person couldn't pay, so the newly-forgiven debtor had him thrown into prison, and turned over to the tormentors, until he could pay back the few dollars. The King learned of the debtor's unconscionable act and called him back in. As a result of the debtor's unwillingness to forgive, he reinstated his debt, threw him in prison, and turned him over to the tormentors until he could repay the un-payable millions of dollars. Verse 35 shows us the dangerous consequence of un-forgiveness: "so likewise shall My heavenly Father do also unto you, if ye from your hearts forgive not every one his brother their trespasses." The result of un-forgiveness is that our debt will be reinstated. Our debt is the debt that Jesus paid on the cross. We will not receive this forgiveness of our sin-debt, and consequently, become separated from God.[1]

Forgiveness means to give up resentment against or to let go of the desire to punish. When you go through painful things at the hands of others, especially being unfairly treated, violated or abused, you tend to feel justified in not forgiving the person responsible for hurting you. But the revelatory truth in Matthew 18:35 paints a sobering picture; when we refuse to forgive, God reinstates our debt and we become like the unforgiving debtor. Unfortunately, this is why so many people go through life feeling tormented in their souls, because they don't know how to, or choose not to forgive. Forgiveness is not always easy, and in some cases it may seem impossible to do, but if we submit to God's Word and rely on His grace, He will lovingly take us

---

[1] Art Mathias, Biblical Foundations of Freedom (Pleasant Valley Publications, 2000)

through the process of forgiveness.

I know from personal experience how un-forgiveness can undermine true worship. Before I developed a relationship with the Lord, I struggled with forgiveness. Whenever someone hurt me, betrayed me or disappointed me, I became angry and held onto it. I was unwilling to forgive, so bitterness and offense took root within my heart. Un-forgiveness quickly became a way of life for me and I lived in a perpetual state of resentment.

As I grew in my relationship with the Lord, I was drawn to worship. At the same time, God began to show me the true state of my heart. Seeing for the first time how dark my heart was, I surrendered myself to God and I asked Him to cleanse me from the inside out. Over the course of one year, God delivered me from the sin of un-forgiveness, and He used His Word to uproot the tentacles of bitterness and resentment from my heart. God even directed me to contact everyone that I was angry with, to repent for harboring un-forgiveness against them. Some of the people that I had to contact were former friends whom I hadn't spoken to in years. There was one person that I was unable to get in touch with because he joined the military and had been deployed. But, when God tells you to do something, He always makes it possible for you to obey. Within days of my desire to speak to my old friend, he actually called me! He told me that he dreamed a dream that I had something to tell him, so he called my parents to find out how to get in contact with me. We were both amazed at God's ability to bring reconciliation in such a supernatural way. I apologized to him and we had a wonderful conversation about the goodness of God.

I cannot express how liberating it was for me to forgive and release everyone. It actually freed my own heart. Prior to being delivered from the sin of un-forgiveness, my worship was limited but I didn't know it. It was only after God delivered me that I began to experience a greater dimension of His presence; that's when I realized that my worship had been restricted because of the condition of my heart.

Un-forgiveness holds you hostage to your pain and casts a dark cloud over your heart. It skews your perspective of God's Word and hinders you from loving others as He commands. Did you know that you demonstrate your love for God by the way in which you love others?

> *"We love because God first loved us. If someone says he loves God, but hates his brother, he is a liar. For he cannot love God, whom he has not seen, if he does not love his brother, whom he has seen. The command that Christ has given us is this: whoever loves God must love his brother also."*
> *–I John 4:19-21 TEV*

The Scripture is clear, whoever loves God must love his brother; it's non-negotiable. This is one of the reasons why un-forgiveness is so damaging, because it undermines our love for God. We can say that we love God, but the proof of our love lies in our choices; are we willing to forgive others for the sake of our relationship with God?

Jesus taught that true forgiveness takes place in your heart; so it is impossible to have a pure heart if you're unwilling to forgive. Un-forgiveness contaminates and taints the heart with anger, bitterness, animosity and hatred, and these pollutants will most certainly prevent you from experiencing the fullness of God's presence.

✠   *"You honor me with your lips but your heart is far from me. Therefore your worship amounts to nothing..."* (Isaiah

29:13)   The implication of this text is that God is not deceived by outer praise that has no inward sincerity. Jesus also quoted this verse to the scribes and Pharisees when He confronted them about their disobedience (Matthew 15:8-9). The scribes and Pharisees were very careful to display an outward show of righteousness, but they did not have an inner devotion to the true commandments of God. They created their own religious traditions that appeared to be righteous, but in reality, they negated the laws of God. It was in this setting that Jesus declared to them that their worship meant nothing.

You can display an outward show of worship and say all of the right things to God but inwardly have no devotion or desire for Him. In other words, you can worship God but not mean it from your heart. What a travesty! That's like giving God a beautifully wrapped gift box with nothing inside of it. God deserves more than that and I believe He's hurt and disappointed when we give Him halfhearted worship. God is not tricked by appearances, so we must be honest with ourselves and remove any façade. It's a waste of time to pretend with God, and we dishonor Him when we deliberately misrepresent our devotion for Him. Worship means nothing to God if there is no sincerity in the worshiper's heart to support it. Thus, we must give God the real thing; genuineness, devotion and love.

Worship is not what you say with your lips; it's what you say with your heart. If your heart does not line up with your worship, then your worship means nothing to God.

✠   *"They that are of a froward heart are an abomination to the Lord..."* (Proverbs 11: 20) A froward heart is a willful heart; one that is stubborn, disobedient and does what it pleases. Jesus linked obedience with love when He said; "If you love me, keep my commandments" (John 14:15). The obvious inference of this scripture is: disobedience proves that we do not love God (at least not according to His set standard). Keep in mind that worship is an expression of love and devotion to God. So, if our love for God is determined by our obedience to God, then it stands to reason that disobedience nullifies our worship.

God's requirement of obedience goes beyond keeping the Ten Commandments; He requires us to follow after His Spirit and not after our flesh (Romans 8:1-2). This means that we are to be led by the Spirit of God (that is within us), and not by our carnal desires. To follow "after the Spirit" is to walk in complete obedience to the leadership of the Holy Spirit, and to walk "after the flesh" is to make your own choices and decisions irrespective of what God desires for you. "And I will put my Spirit within you so that you will obey my laws and do whatever I command." (Ezekiel 36:27 TLB) God has placed His spirit within us so that He can lead us according to His will; which is to build and advance His kingdom here on earth. If we rebel against His spirit, we grieve Him, His kingdom suffers, and we risk missing out on all of the good things that He has for us. God has many blessings for His children but in order to receive them we must serve Him out of an obedient heart. Failure to obey God always results in missed blessings and grave disappointment. "If you are willing and obedient, you will eat the best from the land; but if you resist and rebel, you will be devoured..." (Isaiah 1:19-20 NIV) The Holy Spirit will always let you know if you are violating God's will, but you must be willing to turn and submit yourself to God's authority.

Oftentimes, we naively categorize disobedience by assessing a greater degree of wrongdoing to one form of disobedience versus another, but that is a misleading practice. Blatant disobedience and subtle disobedience are opposite sides of the same coin; even partial obedience is tantamount to disobedience. Some of us even believe that

God overlooks our disobedience if our intentions are good, but there is no evidence in the Bible to support that belief. Unless we fully comply with God's will, our actions fall short of obedience.

Gods' disciplinary action against King Saul reveals that there are consequences for all forms of disobedience. In the Bible's account of his life, we learn that Saul had a willful heart and continually disobeyed God's commands. As a result, he was dethroned and replaced as king over Israel.

In one instance, God commanded King Saul to attack the Amalekite nation and completely destroy everything they had, including the men, women, children, babies, cattle, sheep, camels and donkeys. King Saul and his army attacked the Amalekites, but instead of annihilating the nation, he spared Agag's life (the King of Amalek), and kept the best of the livestock for himself. He destroyed everything else.

God was greatly displeased with King Saul's disobedience, and He told Prophet Samuel that He regretted making Saul king. When Samuel went to see King Saul, Saul cheerfully greeted him and said, "I have carried out the Lord's command!" Samuel challenged his claim by pointing out the cattle noise he heard in the background. King Saul admitted to sparing the best of the livestock, but he argued that he spared them so that he could sacrifice them to God (a form of worship). But his "sacrifice" was a guilt offering to pacify God and cover up his self-seeking motives. Samuel rightly discerned Saul's duplicity and warned him that you cannot placate God with worship. "What is more pleasing to the Lord: your burnt offerings and sacrifices or your obedience to his voice? Obedience is better than sacrifice. Listening to him is much better than offering the fat of rams" (I Samuel 15). In essence, worship is never a substitute for obedience.

Even though Saul feigned ignorance about his actions, and purported himself as an obedient man; the reality is that he was disobedient because he failed to carryout all of God's commands.

Since Saul rejected God's commands, God rejected Saul as king, and He sought after a new king to rule over Israel. When God removed Saul, He replaced him with a man named David; a person whom God said, "is a man after my own heart, for he will obey me." (Acts 13:22 TLB) God chose David to be the new king of Israel because of the character of his heart and his aptitude for obedience. This should prove to us which values are most important to God.

When God began preparing me for ministry, He instructed me to eliminate entertainment from my life so that I could pursue Him without any distractions. Initially I obeyed, but after a while I fell back into my old habits. I even justified my disobedience by telling myself that I needed an outlet to help me unwind after a stressful week at work. I assumed that God agreed with me because He didn't say anything else about it... but I soon found out how wrong I was.

One morning in the middle of my worship, God expressly said to me, "your disobedience has polluted your worship." I was crushed! It was the worst feeling in the world to get reprimanded by God at a moment when I thought He was pleased with me. I had to repent and regroup, but I learned how important obedience is to God.

Disobedience is an insult to God and it shows a lack of respect for His authority. If we want to please God, then we must obey Him; this is the highest form of worship that we can offer. Without obedience, our worship is void, meaningless and completely displeasing to the Lord.

✞   *"I the Lord search the heart; I test the motives to give every man according to his ways"* (Jeremiah 17:10). The motive of your heart is the measure of your worship. God judges the 'why' of what you do and not the 'what' of what you do. What drives you to worship? Do you worship God with an ulterior motive? Are you more focused on what you can get from God than you are with knowing who God really is? Do you worship God for the sake of appearances - to impress those around you with how spiritual you are? Do you go through the motions of worship without making a genuine effort to connect with God?   Do you sing in the choir just to showcase your gift, or desire to be on stage to get acclamation and adulatory praise from others? What is your motive for worship?

There are external factors that can influence and shape your motive for worship. For example, if you grew up in a church where worship was just a traditional part of the service and not a focused time to display love and adoration to God, then your concept of worship is undeveloped. An undeveloped concept of worship will affect your motive. You will find yourself going through the motions but lacking a desire to intimately connect with the heart of God.   In another case, you may be in a church that demonstrates an imbalanced model of worship; they focus entirely on the benefits of it without establishing a true basis for its purpose.   This kind of environment will produce an ulterior motive within your heart, causing you to view worship as a means to *get* from God instead of as a means to *give* to God. This type of mindset will inevitably cause you to be a fair-weather worshiper; one who is ready and eager to worship God when things are going well, but when the storms of life come, you lose your passion and your desire to worship.

During the writing of this book, my family and I had plans to vacation in the Virgin Islands. My dad is a native of St.

Vincent and the Grenadines and we'd never gone as a family to visit his hometown. Growing up, my dad spoke often about one day taking all of us to visit his birthplace; but for various reasons, the trip never materialized. It did, however, remain my dad's fondest desire for many years.

One night at a prayer meeting, through a word of wisdom, it was prophesied to me that God was arranging things for my family and me to take a vacation. Immediately following that prophetic word everything started to fall in place for us to finally take this trip. Sadly, however, at the height of our excitement, a devastating turn of events took place. Less than three weeks before we were scheduled to leave for our trip, my dad was involved in an accident that left him with a severe brain injury.

When I received the call from the hospital, it took me several minutes to comprehend and digest what I was being told. I was in shock, I was confused, and I was scared. How could this happen? Why did this happen? Was my dad going to live or die? I was a wreck. I cried until I became numb. I was like a walking zombie. I could barely function in between the time when I received the news and when I was able to book a flight to go visit my dad.

I didn't know what to do, but I was drawn to worship. So in the middle of the most frightening experience of my life, I began to worship God and I sang like I'd never sung before. I sang at the top of my lungs; "Hail Jesus You're my king, Your life frees me to sing, I will praise you all my days, You're perfect in all Your ways!" The presence of God washed over me and an indescribable peace settled within. In that moment, the spirit of God began moving inside of me, strengthening my inner man and giving me courage to walk through what I was about to face.

When I finally got to the hospital to see my dad, he was in pretty bad shape; his face was swollen and bruised from his injuries, and when he regained consciousness he did not recognize me as his daughter. I became very emotional, but amazingly, my spirit remained stable enough to hear the voice of God. God instructed me to get a Bible and read healing scriptures over my dad. I followed His instructions but there was no immediate change in my dad's condition, (like I had hoped there would be).

The next day I went to church and an unusual thing happened during the service. Towards the end of the sermon, the Holy Spirit began moving and stirring hearts to worship God. So I stood up with my hands lifted, and in that moment I instinctively knew that God wanted me to surrender the outcome of my dad's situation into His sovereign hands. So I released it to God and I renewed my commitment to Him; I affirmed that I would continue serving Him and worshiping Him no matter what happened to my dad...and then I began to sing, "I worship you, Almighty God, there is none like You..."

That same day my mom and I went to the hospital to visit my dad and he had a major breakthrough; he recognized both of us for the first time since his accident. It was incredible. I was blown away by the awesome power of God that was touching my dad right before my eyes.

Due to my dad's age and the severity of his injuries, it's a long uphill climb towards total healing. Yet, I can truly see the hand of God moving on his behalf, and for that, I am eternally grateful.

What seemed like a cruel twist of fate turned out to be an opportunity for me to learn how to persevere in worship. Before my dad's accident I would never have imagined that I could worship through such a difficult frightening experience, but God used my dads' accident to develop that resolve within me. Every true worshiper must acquire the resolve to remain steadfast in worship even in the face of death, or else you'll never be more than a fair-weather worshiper. Your motive will always be off and you won't be able to persevere during the times when worship matters the most.

Having the right worship motive is unquestionably more important to God than the actual act of worship; in fact, God looks past your *act* of worship and performs an assessment test on your heart to determine your true motive.

Tests are designed by God to prove motives. God tested Abraham when He said to him; "Take your son, your only son Isaac, whom you love, and go to the land of Moriah, and offer him there as a burnt offering..." In essence, God told Abraham to go to the place of worship and sacrifice everything. "When they came to the place of which God had told him, Abraham built the altar there and laid the wood in order and bound Isaac his son and laid him on the altar, on top of the wood." Just as Abraham took the knife and reached up to slaughter his son, the angel of God stopped him. "He said, 'Do not lay your hand on the boy or do anything to him, for now I know that you fear God, seeing you have not withheld your son, your only son, from me." (Genesis 22:1-12)

The results of Abraham's test were conclusive; his motive was pure and his commitment to God was rock-solid.

Everyone must pass the motive test to become a true worshiper, because it's the sincerity of your motive that validates your act of worship.

Let me interject this point to clarify the statement I made about

God's testing. There is a distinct difference between a test from God and an attack from the enemy. A test from God will generally challenge your faith, whereas an attack from the enemy is an aggressive situation or a set of circumstances which are detrimental to you and/or your loved ones. God did not cause my dad's accident, but He was able to work in it because I committed it into His hands and chose to trust Him with it. What happened to my dad was clearly an attack from the enemy, but the testimony in it is that God had the final say; He took what the enemy meant for evil and used it for my good.

A Clean Heart

In worship the most valuable offering you can give God is a pure heart, so it is incumbent upon you to rid your heart of all impurities. If any of these pollutants are contaminating your heart, now is the time to deal with it. Cultivating a clean heart is an interactive process between you and God; a process that will surely deepen your level of intimacy with Him. God is the only one with the power to cleanse your heart, but He requires your participation. God does the *supernatural* work of purification, and you are responsible for completing the *natural* work of purification. The space in between the supernatural and the natural is usually a process of time in which God does a work in you that produces fruit of sanctification.

When God was liberating me from the sin of unforgiveness, this one night in particular, I suddenly began weeping uncontrollably. I cried for almost an hour and during that time, I repented to God for the years that I let bitterness and hatred lodge in my heart. Afterwards, I felt cleansed, I felt free and I felt forgiven. What I didn't know then is that while I was crying, God was supernaturally cleansing my heart. In the days and months that followed, God led me to do a number of things that ultimately demonstrated the new state of my heart. As mentioned earlier, God instructed me to contact everyone that I was angry with, to repent for harboring bitterness against them. He also showed me how to biblically respond to people in situations that have the potential to either offend me or anger me. God's grace enabled me to do the natural work of purification, and now my conduct is an outward representation of the supernatural work He did inside of my heart.

God's cleansing process involves a number of important things:

- Repentance
- The Blood of Jesus
- The Word
- Prayer
- Faith
- Obedience
- Counseling (optional)
- Change

Repentance- When your heart is polluted with sin, repentance is required. The main reason why we must repent (to God) for our sins is because un-confessed sin leaves us subject to the penalty of death, as the scripture says; *"the wages of sin is death..."* (Romans 6:23). God is sovereign and His ways are holy, when we violate the sanctity of His Word we must humble ourselves to Him and acknowledge our wrongdoing. *"...for your heart is all wrong in God's sight [it is not straightforward or right or true before God]. So repent of this depravity and wickedness of yours and pray to the Lord, if possible, this contriving thought and purpose of your heart may be removed and disregarded and forgiven you."* (Acts 8:21-22 AMP) When we repent, our sins are erased and blotted out as if they never existed (Acts 3:19). *"If we [freely] admit that we have sinned and confess our sins, He is faithful and just (true to His own nature and promises) and will forgive our sins [dismiss our lawlessness] and [continuously] cleanse us from all unrighteousness [everything not in conformity to His will in purpose, thought, and action]."* (I John 1:9 AMP) Once we confess our sins to God, He forgives us and the cleansing process begins.

The Blood of Jesus- The blood of Jesus carried the power of atonement that reconciled us back to God. In the beginning, man had uninterrupted fellowship and communion with God, but as a result of sin, that fellowship was destroyed. When sin entered into the picture man became eternally separated from the presence of God. At that point, a sacrifice was needed in order to make amends for the sins of man. God chose blood as the acceptable sacrifice: *"...without the shedding of blood there is no forgiveness of sins."* (Hebrews 9:22 TLB) *"For God sent Christ Jesus to take the punishment for our sins and to end all God's anger against us. He used Christ's blood and our faith as the means of saving us from his wrath."* (Romans 3:25 TLB)

The blood has permanently paid the price for all of our past, present, and future sins, and it is the basis whereby God accepts our repentance when we come to Him for forgiveness. *"...the blood of Jesus...cleanses us from every sin."* (I John 1:7 NLT)

The Word- God's Word is referred to as cleansing water, (Ephesians 5:26). When God cleanses us, He primarily uses His Word to wash us clean from all unrighteousness. *"Every scripture is God-breathed (given by His inspiration) and profitable for instruction, for reproof and conviction of sin, for correction of error and discipline in obedience [and] for training in righteousness (in holy living, in conformity to God's will in thought, purpose, and action)..."* (II Timothy 3:16 AMP) The Bible is the only book in the world that addresses every area of life; it shows you where you are, where you need to be, and how to get to where you need to be. Most of your cleansing will come by simply obeying the Word of God.

Research what the Bible says about the issue that's polluting your heart and then allow the Word to be the final authority on that matter. If you submit to the Word, God will give you grace and empower you to act in accordance with His will. *"How shall a young man cleanse his way? By taking heed and keeping watch [on himself] according to Your word [conforming his life to it]."* (Psalms 119:9 AMP)

Prayer- Every level of spiritual growth is achieved through prayer; therefore, it is vital that you under gird your cleansing process with fervent prayer. *"The earnest prayers of a righteous person has great power and wonderful results."* (James 5:16 NLT) Prayer is the vehicle that God uses to enable us to transform our lives; without it, we will not be able to do the cleansing work that God requires.

Through prayer, God will show you the areas of your heart that are not pleasing to Him: *"Search me, O God, and know my heart; test my thoughts. Point out anything you find in me that makes you sad, and lead me along the path of everlasting life."* (Psalms 139:23-24 TLB) Prayer is also how we initiate God's supernatural cleansing; *"Wash me thoroughly from my iniquity, and cleanse me from my sin...create in me a clean heart, O God, and put a new and right spirit within me."* (Psalms 51:2, 10 NRSV) Ultimately, prayer is the key to success because by it, you can receive whatever you need to complete your part of the purification process: *"And this is the confidence which we have in him, that if we ask anything according to his will he hears us. And if we know that he hears us in whatever we ask, we know that we have obtained the requests made of him."* (I John 5:14-15 RSV)

Faith- What is faith? It is to have complete trust and confidence in God. *"...It is the confident assurance that what we hope for is going to happen. It is the evidence of things we cannot yet see."* (Hebrews 11:1 NLT) Faith is essential to your process because there will be times when it appears as if nothing is changing, and during those times, you will have to believe that God is working, even though it seems otherwise. The truth is, from the moment you first pray to God about your heart, He literally begins to work in you (Isaiah 65:24). While God is working, He is equipping you with power to conform your life to His Word. This process does not happen overnight so you can easily become frustrated, and without faith, you may abandon the process before it's complete. God will give you the measure of faith that you need to allow Him to finish His work in you, but you must stand in that faith until the work is done.

If you feel that you have weak faith, there are things you can do to build your faith level. Primarily, the most effective faith building exercise is to audibly speak and declare what the Word of God says about your situation. Faith comes by hearing (Romans 10:17), so as you hear the Word of God that's being spoken out of your mouth, your faith will begin to grow. Another faith building exercise is to study the lives of those who, by faith, accomplished great things for God. This will give you a reference point to help you understand how faith operates. Once you understand how faith operates, you can function in it more successfully. These two exercises are tried-and-true methods for building faith, and utilizing them will cause your faith to grow and become stronger.

Obedience- Your obedience to God's directives throughout your cleansing process will determine how successful you are. You actually jeopardize your progress whenever you fail to act upon what God tells you to do. In this process, you cannot neglect obedience, because depending on what your heart issue is, you may have to take certain actions to finalize your purification.

When I was in the last phase of my cleansing process, I got into a disagreement with a friend about money. The disagreement quickly escalated into a full-blown argument, and in the heat of the moment, callous words were spoken. The facts of our disagreement became grossly distorted and my friend demanded that I pay her a sum of money which I believed I did not owe. I became very angry and vehemently refused her demand. But almost immediately after I decided not to pay the money, I sensed in my heart that God wanted me to forgive my friend and demonstrate His love to her instead of becoming angry. So I humbled myself, and as an act of forgiveness I agreed to pay the money. This was a huge sacrifice for me however, because in addition to not owing the money, I also did not have any disposable income at that time. I was working a part-time job, making minimum wage, and living in a room.

As I was arranging things to be able to pay my friend, the Lord challenged me even more; He instructed me to purchase a gift for her to go along with the money. I agreed to do so, but I had to fight against a lot of negative emotions inside my heart. Nevertheless, I was determined to obey God.

When it came time for me to pay the money, as soon as I gave my friend the gift, my heart was totally freed and all of those negative emotions dissolved. In an instant, the residue of that situation was completely gone and all that I felt in my heart towards my friend was the love of God.

That act of obedience finalized my cleansing process and I got the breakthrough of a lifetime. The heart issue that I had struggled with for most of my life was completely broken. What's more, to my surprise, less than one week later God miraculously restored all of that money back to me. I couldn't believe it. It was the most amazing experience I ever had with God, at that point in my relationship with Him.

Had I not obeyed God I would have probably forfeited my progress and had to redo my process all over again. But because of my obedience, I was completely cleansed and I haven't battled with un-forgiveness ever since that day. And, that was over 11 years ago!

While God is completing His cleansing work in you, I implore you to obey everything He tells you to do, even if some things are difficult for you to carry out. God knows exactly what He's doing, and your obedience to His instructions will produce something remarkable in you.

Counseling- Counseling is certainly not mandatory but it is an option that may be necessary in some situations. For example, you may have suffered a terrible loss caused by an act of violence, or you may have gone through a very bitter divorce, or maybe you were abused as a child. These events (and countless others) create a lot of painful emotions that can eventually turn into bitterness, hatred, and un-forgiveness. If your heart issue is tied to a traumatic experience, then counseling may be a crucial step in your cleansing process. A Pastor or a Christian counselor (which is what I recommend) can be used by God to effectively minister healing and restoration to your soul. They can help you successfully apply the Word of God to your issue, and give you the tools to help you get well and recover.

In the beginning of my cleansing process I saw a counselor, and the help that she gave me was absolutely invaluable. Through the gifts of the spirit (according to I Corinthians 12:7-10), she was able to uncover the root cause of the bitterness I harbored in my heart. While my issue was not caused by a traumatic experience, it had an impetus that was unknown to me. Had it not been for counseling, I would have made little or no progress because I didn't know what my problem was. I needed help to find out why I acted the way that I did. Once the root cause was exposed, it was much easier for me to fulfill my part of the purification process.

If you're struggling to get free in a certain area, you might need some help. Only God knows what you need, so allow the Holy Spirit to confirm whether or not your situation necessitates counseling; and if it does, let God connect you with the right person.

Change- Once your cleansing process is complete, you will undoubtedly have to make some life changes to maintain your new heart. Many times after Jesus delivered someone He said: "go, and sin no more." That was a warning to change, for He was basically saying: go and make some changes or else you will become bound again.

For some, you may have to change your friends, because "bad company corrupts good character." (I Corinthians15:33 NLT) For others, you may be entangled in a relationship that continuously leads you into sin, in which case, you have to end that relationship. In my case, I had to start reacting differently to people who hurt my feelings. In place of becoming angry, I had to choose to release the offense and demonstrate the love of God instead.

You have a responsibility to preserve the state of your new heart, and if you don't change, you run the risk of recontamination. Guard your heart with all diligence and be careful not to do anything that will cause you to return to your former state. Whatever your *change* is, the Holy Spirit will show you what actions you need to take to remain cleansed and free. Remember to listen for His voice and make the necessary adjustments.

Make a commitment to do the work that is needed to improve the condition of your heart. Don't assume that you do not have any issues. There are things inside you that only God can see, and unless He reveals them to you, you may never know the true state of your heart. As you move forward in this process, don't become discouraged by the amount of time it may require, because it's an investment into your development as a worshiper. If you do the work, you will reap a harvest that'll far outweigh your sacrifices.

Summary

As a worshiper, you must allow God to reveal the areas of your heart that do not please Him, and then let Him purify you so that you are fit to enter into His presence. Cleansing your heart will transform you into a vessel of honor and qualify you to offer up true worship to God.

Action Point:

1.   Ask God to search your heart and show you if there is anything in it that does not please Him.

   If you learn that the state of your heart does not meet God's standard of purity, then you must allow Him to cleanse your heart. If you do not let God cleanse your heart, you disqualify yourself from being a true worshiper.

Pray this prayer:

   Dear Heavenly Father, thank You for Your love which is shed abroad in my heart. I acknowledge that I have missed the mark and have fallen short of Your Word. Please forgive me. Search my heart and if You find anything that is not pleasing to You, remove it and cleanse me from all unrighteousness. Sanctify and consecrate me so that I am a vessel of honor for You. I love You and I want to offer You the best worship I can give. Help me to do my part to purify my heart so that the fragrance of my worship truly pleases You. Show me the changes I need to make to align my life with Your Word. As I develop into the type of worshiper You are seeking, help me to never lose my passion and desire for Your presence. Thank You for what You are about to do in me, and may it bring glory to Your name, in Jesus' name, Amen.

III

*It doesn't matter how much you profess
to want God, what matters is what
you do when the rubber meets the road.*

The Anatomy of a Worshiper

"As a deer longs for a stream of cool water, so I long for you, O God. I thirst for you, the living God. When can I go and worship in your presence."
-Psalms 42:1-2 TEV

Throughout the storyline of Scripture, the greatest example of a worshiper is found in the life of King David. David had a relationship with God that was marked by intense passion and profound intimacy. As a man, he was a rare combination of strength and vulnerability; fearless in the face of battle, yet broken and humble in the presence of the Lord. David was known as "a man after God's own heart" and he introduced a style of worship that not only influenced his generation, but it became the standard of worship for which all succeeding generations have aspired.

Arguably the most fascinating character in the Bible, David was the second King of Israel and is famously known for killing the giant Goliath with a single small stone. The story of his life is phenomenally intriguing and includes all of the hallmarks of a best-selling novel: tragedy, triumph, betrayal, scandal, conspiracy, and murder. Not to mention, David was a very handsome, affluent political figure with a vast amount of power and influence. Without a doubt, he would have attracted a whirlwind of media attention if he lived in the 21st century.

David was a man of unparalleled talent and ability; a renowned leader, a valiant warrior, an impressive psalmist, a gifted lyricist, and a consummate worshiper. He was remarkable in every way, but still vulnerable to the temptations that beset most men. Despite his notable achievements, David made significant mistakes which brought about tragic consequences for himself and others. Even so, God preserved him as king and established an elite dynasty from his family lineage.

A forerunner and a trendsetter, David connected with the Lord in a way that had never been done before, and his lifestyle of worship set precedence for the concept of intimacy with God. Upon examining his personal history, we learn that the driving force behind all of his success was his relationship with God. In times of great difficulty, he clung to his faith and did not allow negative circumstances to stop him from pursuing the Lord. He prevailed against every obstacle that came his way and rose to become the most iconic figure in worship history.

One on One

We are first introduced to David as a young Shepherd boy in charge of his father's sheep. As a Shepherd, David's primary responsibilities were to keep his father's flock intact and to protect them from wolves and other dangers. Traditionally, Shepherds lived apart from the general public in order to be in close proximity to their sheep. This made shepherding a very isolated, lonely job. Undoubtedly, this is where David's relationship with God began to develop and take root.

We aren't told much about David's day-to-day activities as

a Shepherd boy but his testimony to King Saul discloses very important information about that season in his life:

"But David said to Saul, 'Your servant has been keeping his father's sheep. When a lion or a bear came and carried off a sheep from the flock, I went after it, struck it and rescued the sheep from its mouth. When it turned on me, I seized it by its hair, struck it and killed it. Your servant has killed both the lion and the bear; this uncircumcised Philistine will be like one of them, because he has defied the armies of the living God. The LORD who delivered me from the paw of the lion and the paw of the bear will deliver me from the hand of this Philistine.'"
-I Samuel 17:34-37 NIV

David learned how to trust in God as a result of what he experienced when he was separated from everyone and everything. This reveals a key principle that is relevant to all worshipers: a period of isolation is necessary for anyone who desires an intimate relationship with God.

When God wants to reveal Himself to you, He will isolate you for a season of time so that He can be alone with you. This season of time is referred to by me as "spiritual isolation."

Many people hate or fear loneliness so they either disdain or misunderstand spiritual isolation. Spiritual isolation is not a curse nor is it a form of cruel and unusual punishment; it is a unique opportunity to focus exclusively on God in order to discover who He really is–His character, His attributes and His divine nature. If God did not separate us during this time, other things would compete for our attention and inevitably distract us from the task at hand.

God separates us so that He can solidify our relationship with Him. Spiritual isolation is designed to be a developmental part of our spiritual growth; if we reject it we inadvertently create a gap in our relationship with the Lord. The only way to establish a real connection with God is to spend time with Him alone. Thus, spiritual isolation should be embraced, not scorned, and we should seek after it instead of attempt to escape it.

The concept of spiritual isolation is best understood when viewed from a natural perspective. For instance, in the Old Testament era, God instructed newly married couples to take a one-year honeymoon, forgoing all responsibilities that would separate them from one another during that time:

> *"If a man has recently married, he must not be sent to war or have any other duty laid on him. For one year he is to be free to stay at home and bring happiness to the wife he has married." —Deuteronomy 24:5 NIV*

God designed a season of isolation for all newlywed couples and He intended this time-frame to be an opportunity for them to focus entirely on getting to know one another physically, emotionally and spiritually. This extended time together gave couples the chance to intimately connect and establish a firm foundation for their marriage. Here we see that the principle of isolation is endorsed by God as an essential part of relationship-building.

Now let's fast forward to the New Testament and take a look at the meaning of marriage:

> *"As the Scriptures say, 'a man leaves his father and mother and is joined to his wife, and the two are united into one.' This is a great mystery, but it is an illustration of the way Christ and the church are one." —Ephesians 5:31-33 NLT*

Marriage is an example of Christ's relationship with the church, illustrating the intensity of His commitment to us, but also indicating the level of intimacy that we are to have with Him. If marriage is meant to be an example of our relationship with Christ then we can take the same command which God gave to newlywed couples and apply it to our relationship with Him.

Another illustration of isolation is found in the life of the apostle Paul. Paul's conversion experience completely transformed his life and ultimately propelled him into the ministry. His account of that event gives us further proof of the legitimacy and effectiveness of spiritual isolation:

"Dear brothers and sisters, I solemnly assure you that the Good News of salvation which I preach is not based on mere human reasoning or logic. For my message came by a direct revelation from Jesus Christ himself. No one else taught me. ...For it pleased God in his kindness to choose me and call me, even before I was born! What undeserved mercy! Then he revealed his Son to me so that I could proclaim the Good News about Jesus to the Gentiles. When all this happened to me, I did not rush out to consult with anyone else; nor did I go up to Jerusalem to consult with those who were apostles before I was. No, I went away into Arabia and later returned to the city of Damascus. It was not until three years later that I finally went to Jerusalem for a visit with Peter and stayed there with him for fifteen days." -Galatians 1:11-12, 15-19 NLT

Paul separated himself from everyone and everything for three years in order to be taught directly by God, and in that season of isolation, his relationship with the Lord flourished. It is evident how truly devoted Paul was to God when we look at how he responded to the trials and tribulations that he encountered thereafter:

"A mob quickly formed against Paul and Silas, and the city officials ordered them stripped and beaten with wooden rods. They were severely beaten, and then they were thrown into prison. The jailer was ordered to make sure

they didn't escape. So he took no chances but put them into the inner dungeon and clamped their feet in the stocks. Around midnight, Paul and Silas began praying and singing hymns to God..." -Acts 16:22-25 NLT

Most of us have never experienced this type of trauma so we can only imagine the agony that Paul must have suffered through. But right in the middle of this painful ordeal, Paul chose to worship. If Paul did not have a solid trust in God he would not have been able to respond to Him the way that he did. Those three years that Paul spent alone with God produced intimacy and divine revelation, a powerful combination that changed the course of his life. Formerly known as a man who oppressed and murdered Christian converts, Paul was once a harsh opponent of the spread of the Gospel. But after becoming intimate with God his mind was radically changed and his life's purpose was realized. He went from being a man who inflicted suffering on others, to a man who counted it a privilege to suffer for Christ. What Paul received from God during those three years of isolation impacted him so greatly that he was able to endure hardships and intense persecutions without ever becoming offended at God. He remained faithful to his calling and finished his course.

Had there been a gap in Paul's relationship with God he would have never been able to withstand all of the adversities that he had to go through to fulfill his God-given purpose.

Spiritual isolation is a priceless season of time designed by God to establish a firm foundation for our relationship with Him, to closely knit our hearts together with his, and to prepare us for our destiny. Without the discipline of spiritual isolation we will never develop the focus and commitment necessary to fulfill our God-given purpose. We will either get distracted by the cares of this world or become mislead by the lust of the eyes and the pride of life.

Many of us live in a culture where everything is designed

to cater to our flesh, as a result, we've become robust by things that lack spiritual substance. If we don't take heed to God's call for isolation we will go through life with malnourished spirits, sedated by an escapist mentality.

There are all types of options and voices that carry a subliminal message which suggest there's something wrong with being alone. Have you ever wondered why that is? Why is there such a negative stigma associated with being alone? I believe it's because the adversary wants to keep us in constant fear of loneliness so that we won't desire to be alone with God. He generates the fear, which in turn causes us to do everything we can to prevent ourselves from being alone. It's a spiritual attack designed to keep us from knowing God for ourselves. This is not a subtle attack either. For example, social media is wildly popular, in part, because it provides an alternative to being alone. With the advent of social media we have a myriad of websites at our disposal that enable us to connect and socialize with anyone, anywhere anytime. It takes no real effort to escape the discomfort of being alone. My contention is that the adversary overtly uses modern technology to over stimulate our appetite for social interaction so that we don't regard or esteem spending time alone with God.

I am not advocating antisociality; God made us social beings so there is nothing wrong with socializing. Social interaction plays a huge role in our psychological development and therefore, is a valid human necessity. However, there will be times in your life when God will remove people from your life and/or put you in a position where you're all by yourself. But if you fear loneliness and don't understand the purpose of isolation, you'll run from God and miss a critical part of your spiritual development.

I've personally experienced the joys and sorrows of spiritual isolation. I lived by myself for a number of years and that timeframe became my season of isolation. The Lord picked that time in my life to pull me away from everything so that He could do a work in me. As a result, I had to give up most of the recreational activities that I normally enjoyed, including entertainment, leisure travel and attending various social events. It was a very difficult sacrifice to make and at times, I truly hated it. But when it was all said and done, that was the most productive season of my life. During that time, I discovered within myself a hidden passion for worship and I experienced God at levels I never knew were possible. God revealed to me His purpose for my life and showed me the gifts and talents that He placed inside me. He even birthed a worship ministry in me and led me to write this book. None of these things could have happened outside of spiritual isolation.

God draws all of His children into seasons of isolation, times where He separates us from everyone and everything so that He can be alone with us. In turn, He wants us to willingly come away from the trappings of life and earnestly desire to be alone with Him. He doesn't want to be an afterthought at the end of our day or play second fiddle to the things we'd rather be doing. He wants us to acknowledge our need for a close relationship with Him and then create a space in our life that's reserved just for His presence.

God's isolation methods are very diverse; He does not use a cookie cutter system or apply a one-size-fits-all technique. If He did, everyone would not be able to participate in it because our lives are vastly different from each other. A single woman with no children has a lot more availability than a working mother of five. So, God, in His infinite wisdom, uniquely designs each person's isolation period and gives us individualized plans that will fit our schedule and our lifestyle. For example, God may tell a single woman with no children to dedicate her season of singleness exclusively to Him, spending the majority of her time seeking His face. While on the other hand, He may tell a working mom of five to wake up an hour before her family and retreat downstairs to her basement to be alone with Him. Everyone's season of isolation will look different but it will produce the same results.

Bear in mind, your season of isolation may initially be uncomfortable and require sacrifice. You may have to wrestle with the fear of being alone, or you may have to struggle with letting go of certain things. But whatever your challenge may be, if you push through it, you will connect with God and grow to appreciate being alone with Him.

There's no substitute for spending time alone with God, it's a necessary rite of passage in our development as true worshipers.

Now, back to David...

David learned to trust in God because while he was alone in the field, whenever anything came against him, God rescued him and delivered him out of trouble. Have you ever thought about what David might have done if his family were in the field with him? More than likely he would have cried out to them for help, as that would have been the logical thing to do. But, can you see how God would not have had the opportunity to reveal Himself to David if David were not isolated from everyone and everything?

Isolation was probably very difficult for David. We can reasonably assume that he would have rather been with his family, enjoying a normal life, eating supper at the dinner table each night. As the youngest boy, I'm sure David admired his older brothers and would have preferred to spend time with them instead of being all by himself in the field. But, when it came time to kill Goliath, it was clear that David had something in him that his brothers did not have.

Goliath was a Philistine, and history tells us that the Philistines were archenemies of the Israelites. He stood over nine feet tall and was understandably very frightening to look upon. One day, he began to harass the Israelite army:

"Goliath stood and shouted to the ranks of Israel, "Why do

you come out and line up for battle? Am I not a Philistine, and are you not the servants of Saul? Choose a man and have him come down to me. If he is able to fight and kill me, we will become your subjects; but if I overcome him and kill him, you will become our subjects and serve us." Then the Philistine said, "This day I defy the ranks of Israel! Give me a man and let us fight each other." On hearing the Philistine's words, Saul and all the Israelites were dismayed and terrified...When the Israelites saw the man, they all ran from him in great fear."
-I Samuel 17:8-11, 24

David's brothers were in Saul's army (I Samuel 17:13), which meant they were skilled warriors with years of combat experience. Yet, they were terrified of Goliath and ran from him just like everyone else did. What a striking contrast to how David -the shepherd boy- responded when he encountered Goliath:

"David said to Saul, 'Let no one lose heart on account of this Philistine; your servant will go and fight him'...then he took his staff in his hand, chose five smooth stones from the stream, put them in the pouch of his shepherd's bag and, with his sling in his hand, approached the Philistine...as the Philistine (Goliath) moved closer to attack him, David ran quickly toward the battle line to meet him. Reaching into his bag and taking out a stone, he slung it and struck the Philistine on the forehead. The stone sank into his forehead, and he fell facedown on the ground."
-I Samuel 17:32, 40, 48-49

The distinction between someone who spends time alone with God is poignantly clear in this example. In the field of isolation, David experienced God. He saw Him as a mighty deliverer, a covenant keeper, a trustworthy protector, and a powerful force to be reckoned with. His brothers were at a disadvantage because they did not take time to be alone with God to build a relationship with Him. As a result, they did not know God. When Goliath came against David's brothers, none of them had the boldness, the courage, or the faith in God that David had.

The foundation of David's relationship with the Lord was built on trust, and from that place of trust a worshiper was born. David fell deeply in love with God as a result of learning about Him firsthand. The experiences that David had with the Lord (in the field of isolation), left an indelible mark on his heart and led him to pen some of the most beautiful words ever written about God.

A worship relationship with God is developed in private; in the "secret place" is where you establish a heart-to-heart connection with Him. This is why spiritual isolation is so important, because it creates a space for us to truly discover God.

Pursuit

David's first interaction with King Saul came when the spirit of the Lord departed from Saul. As a result of his disobedience, the Lord lifted His hand from upon Saul and sent a tormenting spirit against him. One of Saul's servants recognized that he was being tormented by an evil spirit, so he suggested that Saul get a skilled musician so that whenever the evil spirit came upon him, the musician would play and the evil spirit would depart. The servant recommended David, Saul agreed, and David was brought before the King. King Saul took an immediate liking to David, so much so that he invited him to remain in the palace as his personal musician and armor-bearer.

King Saul was very impressed with David's victory against Goliath and this prompted him to appoint David as commander over his army. David was successful every time he went to battle because the hand of the Lord was upon him. With every victory he achieved, his notoriety increased throughout all of Israel. As time progressed however, something evil began brewing in Saul's heart. David's success started to eclipse Saul's popularity, and as a result, Saul became very jealous. He felt threatened by David and feared that David would one day take the kingdom away from him.

David was anointed by Prophet Samuel to be the next King of Israel, so he probably thought that God placed him in the palace to be mentored and trained by Saul. But destiny had another plan. Instead of Saul taking him under his wings and showing him the ropes, Saul's jealousy turned him into a homicidal maniac. In a twisted turn of events, Saul went off the deep end and began making attempts on David's life.

David had no other choice but to flee the palace to save himself. So with the help of Saul's son Jonathan, David escaped the King's wrath, but he did so with a great deal of sadness in his heart. David was loyal to Saul; he revered him and esteemed it an honor to serve in his palace. So when Saul's wrath turned on him, he was confused and distraught.

After David fled the palace Saul launched a vigorous search effort to hunt him down and kill him. Saul viewed David as a threat to his kingdom and he wanted him permanently eliminated. Consequently, David was forced into exile and lived as a fugitive for many years of his life. This pursuit became the backdrop for David's development as a warrior, a psalmist, and a worshiper, and it was God's training ground to prepare him for his destiny as the next King of Israel.

In the course of his flight, David gained the support of about 600 men; men who were in distress, in debt and bitter in soul gathered themselves to him and he became captain over them, (I Samuel 22:2). They traveled from place to place, and one day news came to David that the Philistines were in the city of Keilah stealing grain from the threshing floors. So David asked the Lord, "should I go and attack them?" God gave David the green light and David and his men went to Keilah and he led them in victory against the Philistines.

When Saul learned that David was in Keilah he summoned all of his men to go down to Keilah to besiege him. But David knew that Saul was plotting harm against him so he and his men fled Keilah and went into the wilderness. From that point on, Saul hunted for him every single day.

With the threat of destruction looming over his head, David was constantly on the run for his life; sneaking around from place to place, sleeping in caves and using stones as pillows to rest his head. To no fault of his own he found himself in a season of great distress. In spite of these trying conditions however, David's connection with God remained secure. At this juncture, he was no longer in the honeymoon phase of their relationship, but his desire for God did not wane. Throughout the entire season that Saul chased after him, David pursued the presence of God with all of his might. He did not allow adversity to stop him from seeking after the Lord. This reveals another key principle which I believe applies to all *true* worshiper's: the principle of pursuit.

> *"Though a host should encamp against me, my heart shall not fear: though war should rise against me, in this will I be confident. One thing have I desired of the LORD, that will I seek after; that I may dwell in the house of the LORD all the days of my life, to behold the beauty of the LORD, and to inquire in his temple." -Psalms 27:3-4*

In essence, David was saying to God: I want to be with you more than anything and I will look for you, search for you and try to find you, hunt for you, seek you out, ask for you, inquire about you and request to be with you *until* I find you.

The principle of pursuit is a spiritual law designed by God to be the means by which we discover Him:

> *"You will seek me and find me when you seek me with all*

your heart." -Jeremiah 29:13 NIV

As worshipers, our desire for God should compel us to pursue Him. If we say that we want God but are not inclined to seek after Him, our "desire" for Him is insincere.

The art of pursuit lies within each of us, everyone everywhere is pursuing something. Whether you're pursuing a career, an education, a mate, etc...all of us can identify with the concept of pursuit. Consider, if you will, the amount of time and effort it takes to become a doctor. One would have to complete 4 years of undergraduate education, followed by 4 years of medical school, and then another 4 years of residency work. That's a 12-year commitment that requires sustained focus throughout; including countless hours of studying and preparing for medical exams, extensive research and writing assignments, and a grueling on the job training program, not to mention overcoming every obstacle and every setback that may arise along the way. It takes a significant amount of self-discipline, resilience and strength of mind to achieve your medical license, because the preparation time is stressful, demanding and exhausting. Yet, people from all walks of life manage to achieve this accomplishment year after year - all because they have a *desire* to practice medicine. Now consider the level of desire you would have to possess to be willing to go through the arduous process of becoming a doctor. That is the minimum level of desire you and I should have in our pursuit for God. We have to want Him more than anything and we must be willing to go through whatever it takes to be with Him.

Desire determines pursuit; how badly you want something predicts what you're willing to go through to get it.

The principle of pursuit suggests perseverance and determination; it means you never give up. For David, being with God far surpassed anything he had ever experienced, and as a result, he wanted more. He yearned for God's presence and the difficult circumstances that he went through did not diminish his passion nor deter his pursuit.

Many of us start off strong in our relationship with God, but when problems arise or when disruptive events transpire in our lives, we back off and lose our zeal. Once we lose our zeal, our focus shifts and our commitment declines. Pursuit requires commitment. David was completely displaced and his life hung in the balance, yet he managed to remain committed to pursuing God. The mayhem and turmoil that turned his life upside down did not overshadow his desire to be with God.

Understand that we live in a fallen world therefore, trials and tribulations are par-for-the-course. We must settle in our minds that negative circumstances will inevitably occur in our lives; families may break apart, loved ones may pass away, tragedies may befall us, and catastrophic events may happen around us. But the issue is not about the things that happen to us, the issue is about maintaining our connection to God regardless of our circumstances.

We live in this world but we're not of it, our citizenship is in heaven and our natural habitation is the presence of God, that's where we originated from. Every living organism is designed to exist and thrive within its natural habitat; if it's detached from where it belongs it will eventually wither away and die. During that detachment period, however, it will seek to return to its natural environment until survival is no longer possible. Herein lies the crux of our pursuit, it is a journey back to where we belong.

Have you ever seen fish being removed from their tanks? They splatter and flail around desperate for water. That's a picture of how our spirits respond to being outside of the presence of God. This is what David was experiencing when he wrote:

> *"God, you are my God, earnestly I seek you; my soul thirsts for you, my body longs for you, in a dry and weary land where there is no water." -Psalms 63:1 NIV*

David was desperate to return to the place where he belonged, the place where his spirit thrived. He knew that if his spirit was strong he could withstand the negative circumstances in his physical environment.

In the presence of God we transcend this world and all of its hurt, pain and injustice. And as a result of being in God's presence, we're infused with grace that enables us to endure our conflicts and rise above the storms of life. His presence is what makes the difference.

By and large, we pursue things motivated by a reward for success. That's not a negative thing, it's a fact. We innately or instinctively expect to be rewarded for our accomplishments in life. After all, it would be foolish not to expect some type of return after investing our time and resources into an endeavor. God created us with this expectation because it reflects the manner in which He operates. God is a "rewarder" of those who diligently seek Him, (Hebrews 11:6). Think about the highest achievement you can attain and the corresponding reward for that achievement. That "reward" doesn't even measure up to what God is capable of giving you.

A part of our incentive for pursuing God is the fact that He will reward our pursuit. Look at how God rewarded David; he became the most successful prominent figure of his time and was chosen to be a part of the lineage of Jesus Christ. Truly God will abundantly compensate us for seeking after Him, even restoring back to us anything we may lose along the way. Our greatest reward, of course, is His presence. God's presence is the only place that exists which offers fullness of joy and pleasures forevermore. This is why the Word says; "better is one day in your courts than a thousand elsewhere" (Psalms 84:10). We may derive joy from our personal pursuits in life, but it's a fractional joy. We may even find pleasure in the things of this world, but it's transitory and will not last. The only lasting pleasure in life comes from the joy that we receive from being with God. Sadly, however, many of us will devote the prime of our lives seeking other things for pleasure, only to find – in the end – that we missed out on the true joy of life.

Pursuing God is a lifetime venture; it never ends because God has no end. There are infinite realms, countless dimensions and multiple layers of God; no one could ever fully discover the many facets of His deity. In God's presence we soar from one level of glory to the next, we never stop ascending, never stop discovering and never stop experiencing the magnificence of who He is. In turn, God never stops revealing the wonders of His glory to us. It is an exquisite delight to fellowship with God at this level and there is no greater adventure in life than to explore the realms of His glorious presence. There is, however, a divine qualifier that we must meet for God to unveil Himself to us in such a magnitude, and that is: we have to be diligent in our pursuit. God is looking for consistency and passion. It takes time to demonstrate your desire (for God) and to establish yourself as a true worshiper. As much as we may want it to, it does not happen overnight. If we achieved the glory realm with minimal desire and little effort we would take it for granted and would not be able to appreciate its value.

Years ago a friend and I both got brand new cars around the same time. I purchased mine and her dad purchased hers. Almost immediately it was apparent that we both had two different levels of appreciation for our cars; I carefully followed the manufacturer's maintenance recommendations and routinely took my car to be serviced, and always made sure that it was clean, inside and out. My friend, on the other hand, was not as meticulous with the maintenance of her car. She only took it to be serviced whenever the engine light came on and she almost never washed it. Within three years her car developed several problems and its appearance began to fade. At the same time my car still looked new and was in perfect driving condition. I cherished my car because prior to getting it I either had to ride the bus or carpool with someone in order to get to where I wanted to go. I wanted a car so badly, it was all I talked about, worked towards and prayed for for almost two years. Conversely, my friend did not have to struggle or work to get a car; she simply turned 18 and one was given to her. As a result, her car had very little value to her; she didn't appreciate it because she didn't earn it. Instant gratification of any kind is damaging to our spiritual growth because we are not designed to receive fulfillment without investment and sacrifice. When we attain anything of value with no real effort it is impossible to appreciate its worth.

Appreciation is a byproduct of pursuit; we need to exert our time and energy into pursuing God in order to appreciate His presence once we finally encounter it.

Pursuit has more than one phase; the first phase is usually very tentative, similar to the beginning stages of a courtship in which longevity is questionable. Time will test your commitment and prove whether or not your desire is real. Inherent in every pursuit is a crossroad–a point in time where we have to decide if what we're seeking after is really worth the effort, a time where we'll either quit or resolve to continue moving forward in spite of the sacrifices. What we do at our crossroad determines what God does next. If we don't maintain our commitment at this point, God will not unveil His glory to us. It's not that He doesn't want to, rather, it's because our lack of commitment reveals a truth that was hidden beneath the surface all along: we don't really want Him.

Persistent pursuit is the only way to establish credibility as a true worshiper. It doesn't matter how much you profess to want God, what matters is what you do when the rubber meets the road. Are you truly willing to lay everything else aside and focus on pursuing God until you breakthrough, or is "pursuit" just something you pay lip service to? Most of us talk a good game but in actuality lack the discipline to really follow-through with pursuing God. We squander away our time on people and things that ultimately distract us from ever getting serious with God, and we put Him on the backburner of life and continue living the status quo. The reality is we're content just having a mediocre relationship with God even though we know there's so much more. With such apathy permeating the Body of Christ is there any wonder *why* God has to look for worshipers? He searches them out because true worshipers are rare and hard to find. God is looking for worshipers that are earnestly seeking Him, worshipers that have paid the price of perseverance. He wants worshipers that will pursue His glory until they uncover realms of worship that have not been unveiled yet. Yes, there are dimensions of worship that have not been discovered yet, but the question is: who is taking the time to seek them?

There is unlimited discovery potential in the realms of God's glory but we must be willing to go beyond the rudimentary aspects of worship to get to those undisclosed realms. David was consumed with a desire for God and that "desire" drove him to pursue God relentlessly. Out of that pursuit emerged an expression of worship that was revolutionary and groundbreaking. In his day, the people were not worshiping God in song and they had not been predisposed to the concept of intimacy with God. Their method of worship was centered on the Ark of the Covenant, which at that time was symbolic and representative of the presence of God. This "presence of God" was not disclosed to the masses but kept behind a veil and only accessible to a select group of people known as the High Priests. As an act of worship, the people were required to bring an offering to the High Priest. The High Priest then took their offering, went behind the veil and worshiped God on their behalf. This was more-or-less the worship model that everyone practiced during David's era. So when David began singing to God, it was an organic expression of worship that originated from his heart. At a time when no one "seemingly" had the means to intimately commune with God, David's desire for God drove him to test the limits. He broke away from the mold and did not let the cultural standard of worship define his relationship with God.

In our generation, we face the same challenge that David did in his. The church has adopted a formulaic style of worship that is conducive to ritualistic behaviors rather than relationship building with God. We've incorporated the pattern of David's worship but not the spirit of worship that drove him to pursue the presence of God. As a result, we've produced a method of worship that is almost completely void of personal authenticity.

True pursuit moves you beyond religious barriers and causes you to develop your own expression of worship. It takes you out of your comfort zone and drives you to seek God until you come face-to-face with Him for yourself. If you want to get to those undisclosed realms, you cannot get boxed into a methodology of worship. Worship must be an open forum of spontaneity ever evolving and ever progressing towards the new (Isaiah 42:10). Just like David, we cannot allow man's traditions to place parameters on our worship, and we can't rely on tradition to secure our connection with God. We each are responsible for building our own relationship with God and it's up to us to take advantage of the access we have to His presence. Pursuit is a choice and God does not legislate our choices. We have to decide what matters most to us and then go after it. God wants us to choose Him just as He chose us and He wants us to want Him just as He wants us. He's given us a glimpse of His glory and now beckons us to pursue Him for more. The more we seek Him, the more we experience Him, and the more we experience Him, the more we want Him. This is the essence of true pursuit.

Brokenness & Contrition

After spending years as a fugitive, the pieces of David's life finally fell into place. Saul was killed in battle at the hand of an enemy and shortly thereafter David was crowned king. Under David's administration, Israel became an independent nation and exponentially expanded her borders. David successfully fought wars against Israel's neighbors resulting in the establishment of an empire that extended over both sides of the Jordan River. He divided the country into twelve districts, each with its own civil, military and religious institutions.[1] His strategic course of action and flawless command made him a leader of great renown. He achieved critical acclaim and won the support of kings and dignitaries from the surrounding nations.

This was an amazing time for David; the world was at his feet. He had power, wealth, and success. He was a military genius, a political titan and well on his way to becoming a global icon. It was impossible to imagine that anything could ever undermine his fame. What could weaken a man who was undefeatable in battle and conquered every obstacle that came his way? David would soon find out. At the height of his popularity his personal life took an unexpected turn for the worst, causing David to discover that his greatest nemesis was none other than himself. In one of the most infamous crimes ever recorded in bible history, David sinned against God and engaged in very unscrupulous behavior. The recount of the incident literally reads like a modern day Hollywood movie script.

> *"And it came to pass, after the year was expired, at the time when kings go forth to battle, that David sent Joab, and his servants with him, and all Israel; and they destroyed the children of Ammon, and besieged Rabbah. But David tarried still at Jerusalem." -II Samuel 11:1*

According to scripture this was a time when David should have been on the battlefield, but for reasons unknown, he sent others out on his behalf and he remained at home. At this point, we know David is not fulfilling the duties of his office, so it is reasonable to assume that he had a lot of extra time on his hands, perhaps meandering around the house in search of something to do. One evening while he was on the roof of his palace, he looked across the courtyard and saw a very beautiful woman bathing. Aroused by feelings of lust, he quickly began to

---

[1] www.preceden.com, Abraham Through Modern Day Israel Timeline

inquire about the identity of this woman. "Is not this Bathsheba the daughter of Eliam, the wife of Uriah the Hittite?" (II Samuel 11:3)   His servant intentionally revealed that Bathsheba was a married woman to deter David from pursuing her.   But David ignored Bathsheba's marital status–treating it as nothing more than an inconsequential detail. Knowing that her husband Uriah was on the battlefield, David saw an opportunity to go after her. So he sent messengers to Bathsheba's house and invited her over to his palace.

Responding to David's invitation, Bathsheba went to the palace to meet him. One thing led to another, and they ended up having a one night stand. Afterward, they both went back to their respective lives and assumed their tryst would remain a secret. But, they soon found out that what's done in the dark always comes to light, (Luke 8:17). Bathsheba discovered that she was pregnant with David's child, and things quickly went from bad to worse.   News of Bathsheba's pregnancy triggered a series of events that had deadly repercussions and caused irreparable damage to David's life and ministry.

In an elaborate attempt to cover up his sin, David devised a plan to make it look as if Uriah impregnated Bathsheba. He recalled Uriah from the battlefield and summoned him to the palace. His intention was to create an opportunity for Uriah to sleep with Bathsheba, but his plan backfired because Uriah had a code of ethics that he would not break. Uriah refused to eat, drink or be intimate with his wife while his fellow soldiers were still at war sleeping in the open field. Clearly, this was an honorable man, one who was loyal and faithful to the cause, the exact type of soldier that made David's army so successful. But unfortunately, David couldn't see Uriah's worth because he was blinded by the deceitfulness of his own corrupt motives.

After his plan failed David conspired to have Uriah killed. So he sent Uriah back to the battlefield and had him placed on the frontline where the fighting was the fiercest. He then arranged for the lead soldier to abandon Uriah so that he wouldn't have any protection when the warfare intensified. As a result, Uriah was struck down and killed in the heat of battle. David not only plotted Uriah's death, he also made it look as if Uriah was just a normal casualty of war. No one suspected a thing and David's life continued on as normal, his image and reputation completely intact.

Immediately following Uriah's death, David married Bathsheba and moved her into his palace in preparation for the birth of their child. Their happiness was short-lived, however, because David's day of reckoning came swiftly and unawares. God was terribly displeased with David for his wicked misdeeds, so He sent a prophet to pronounce judgment upon him.

"So the Lord sent the prophet Nathan to tell David this story: 'There were two men in a certain city, one very rich, owning many flocks of sheep and herds of goats; and the other very poor, owning nothing but a little lamb he had managed to buy. It was his children's pet, and he fed it from his own plate and let it drink from his own cup; he cuddled it in his arms like a baby daughter. Recently a guest arrived at the home of the rich man. But instead of killing a lamb from his own flocks for food for the traveler, he took the poor man's lamb and roasted it and served it.'"
-II Samuel 12:1-4 TLB

David was enraged at the rich man's lack of pity for the poor man, so he decreed to Nathan that the rich man should be killed and the poor mistreated man should be restored four times over. Nathan's response hit David like a ton of bricks:

"Then Nathan said to David, 'You are that rich man! The Lord God of Israel says,' 'I made you king of Israel and saved you from the power of Saul. I gave you his palace and his wives and the kingdoms of Israel and Judah; and if that had not been enough, I would have given you much,

much more. Why, then, have you despised the laws of God and done this horrible deed? For you have murdered Uriah and stolen his wife. Therefore murder shall be a constant threat in your family from this time on because you have insulted me by taking Uriah's wife. I vow that because of what you have done, I will cause your own household to rebel against you. I will give your wives to another man, and he will go to bed with them in public view. You did it secretly, but I will do this to you openly, in the sight of all Israel.'" -II Samuel 12:7-12 TLB

So David admitted to Nathan that he sinned against the Lord, and Nathan said to him:

"...Yes, but the Lord has forgiven you, and you won't die for this sin. But you have given great opportunity to the enemies of the Lord to despise and blaspheme him, so your child shall die." -II Samuel 12:13-14 TLB

Shortly thereafter Bathsheba gave birth to their child and the word of the Lord was fulfilled. Almost immediately the baby became deathly ill. In response, David threw himself at the mercy of God and begged for his child's life to be spared. He fasted and prayed for seven days, but to no avail. God's judgment would not be reversed. On the seventh day, the baby died. When David learned that his child passed away, he got up, took a shower, changed his clothes and went to the Tabernacle to worship God.

There are many theologians and bible scholars that have penned a myriad of in-depth commentaries about this particular juncture in David's life. I'm not here to dispute or support any of their view points because that's not the issue at hand. The issue is how we as worshipers should handle our sins.

Most of us have a hard time believing that a man so close to God could be capable of such dishonorable behavior. But the truth is, everyone's carnal nature is prone to sin if given the opportunity. This entire chapter of David's life could have been avoided had he remained focused on God and obedient to his call. David's fatal error was that he took his eyes off of his God-ordained purpose. In a very real sense, he moved himself out of the will of God by not remaining faithful to what He was called to do. At that point, he became an open target for the enemy. We must realize that lack of focus is a carnal motivation that always gives the adversary an opportunity to attack our destiny. This is precisely what happened to David.

As worshipers, our primary objective is to preserve the strength of God's presence in our lives, regardless of what state we find ourselves in. In the case of sin, nothing separates us from God more deeply than our own personal transgressions. For this reason, it is critical that we swiftly and appropriately address our sin(s) with God. Fortunately, this period of David's life provides a blueprint for how to do that.

Perhaps the most vital lesson we must learn is how to correctly respond when our sin is exposed. Notice how David reacted when Nathan confronted him about his sin:

"And David said unto Nathan, I have sinned against the LORD." -II Samuel 12:13

To his credit, David instantly took responsibility for his actions. One might not see this as an important fact, but I assure you it is. The scandals that flood the front pages of our newspapers prove that most of us do not take ownership of our mistakes. When it comes time for us to face up to our bad behavior we generally become defensive and use others as scapegoats to shift the blame onto. Rarely do we see people admit they're wrong and then deal with the consequences head on.

In the previous chapter, I shared how I disobeyed God by not eliminating entertainment from my life. The second part of that story is a lot more humbling (for me) than the first half. Due to my own disobedience I went through a very bitter season. Somewhere in the middle of that season I became angry with God for not stopping me from making such a bad mistake. After all, He's God, why didn't He prevent me from doing something that He knew would cause me so much pain. My anger indirectly put up a wall between me and God, and from that place, our intimacy hung in the balance. To be very candid, I withheld my worship from God because I wanted to hurt Him. In my mind, He had let me down and I wanted to punish Him for that. I often ask myself how I got to that place. How did I muster up the audacity to actually blame God for my own rebellion? How could I even go there when in my heart I truly loved Him and I knew that He loved me? The truth is, when we choose not to own up to our sins, we're in danger of getting caught up in a warped sense of reality; and once that happens, it is very easy to turn on God.

I had backed myself into a corner and the only way out was to take responsibility for my actions. The only way out was to repent and accept the consequences for the poor choices that I made. So I humbled myself and went before God. I thought I would have to pay some sort of penance to win back His favor, but to my surprise, He was waiting for me with open arms. It was a joyous relief to discover that God had not turned away from me, even though I turned away from Him. I am so thankful that His love for me is not as shaky as my love often is for Him.

Next, David demonstrates what God requires from us when we're dealing with our sins:

"The sacrifice you want is a broken spirit. A broken and repentant heart, O God, you will not despise."
-Psalms 51:17 NLT

Repentance, for most Christians, is a logical response to sin. However, there's much more to repentance than just telling God you're sorry. True repentance is first and foremost an attitude of the heart. Are you truly sorry or are you just sorry that you got caught. Anyone can say the words "I'm sorry" but not everyone regrets their bad behavior. When David's sin was exposed he was devastated.   His heart was filled with sorrow because he transgressed against his God. He was remorseful and deeply troubled by his actions. This pleased God.

> *"For godly sorrow worketh repentance...*"
> -II Corinthians 7:10

God uses sorrow to help us turn away from sin. Without sorrow, there can be no true repentance.

Sin creates a breach in your fellowship with God and a true worshiper will not be able to bear that breach. That is why David responded the way he did, he could not stand the thought of being separated from God for any length of time. When Nathan exposed his sin, what concerned David the most was that his ability to access God's presence was at risk. He knew that he had to get his heart right with God to protect the intimacy they shared. So he cried out:

> *"Create in me a clean heart oh God and renew a right spirit in me.   Do not banish me from your presence... forgive me, and then I will joyfully sing of your forgiveness. Unseal my lips, oh Lord, that I may praise you."*
> -Psalms 51:10-15

If you honestly take responsibility for your sins, without making excuses or looking for someone to blame, Godly sorrow will take root within you and produce true repentance in your heart.

Finally, and equally important, is that we must fully accept the consequences for our sins. Jesus, our Savior, took away the ultimate consequence for our sins (on the cross), so we do not walk in condemnation nor do we have to pay the price for our sins. However, sometimes our disobedience takes us down a difficult road that we would have otherwise not been on had we obeyed God. Or, sometimes our disobedience causes us to miss a blessing that God had in store for us. Of course God will restore what we missed, but in the meantime, we may have to endure some challenges while He works out His plan of restoration. Worship does not absolve us from these types of consequences, but God's grace is sufficient enough to help us deal with the consequences head on.

In David's case, the consequence for his sin was terribly tragic, (I don't believe this type of consequence would befall a New Testament Christian, because we have Grace that was not available in the Old Testament law that David was under). When he learned that his baby was ill, he employed every spiritual measure that he knew of to try and reverse God's judgment. He desperately wanted to keep his child alive but sadly, in spite of everything he tried, the baby died. David's reaction (to his child's death) clearly reveals that he completely accepted the consequences for his sin. Immediately after his baby's death, he went to the Tabernacle to worship God. Without a doubt, this was a defining moment in David's walk with the Lord because this tragedy could have destroyed their relationship. He could have very easily become angry with God for not sparing his child's life, but he didn't. He took ownership for his mistakes and held himself solely responsible for the fallout. He didn't turn away from God not even for a moment. The worship relationship he built with God was strong enough to withstand the worst day of his life. What a testament to the strength of the connection that he shared with God.

The proof, as to whether or not you truly accept the consequences for your actions, lies in your worship. If you're able to continue worshiping God throughout the consequences you have to bear, you can rest assured you're not holding Him accountable for your mistakes. If you can reaffirm your love for God when the pressure is the greatest, you will make it to the other side with your worship relationship intact. This is what separates the wheat from the tares in worship. If your relationship with God is built on anything other than your love for Him, you won't make it through this phase. You must realize that true worship is not for the faint of heart. It's for mature followers of Christ, and you have to decide which one you want to be. Are you going to use your mistakes as an excuse to stop pursuing the Lord? The truth is we all will make mistakes and fall short of God's glory, but there is grace to help us get back up and continue moving forward. If we wallow in self-pity over what we lost or what we missed our hearts will grow cold and we will eventually turn away from God.

David knew the value of having God's presence in his life; it was worth more to him than his wealth, his fame, his image or his prestige. Nothing he possessed measured up to the love that he found in God. Is this your testimony?

Summary

To cement a solid connection with God you must spend time with him alone, pursue him relentlessly and never allow your sins to separate you from Him. If you focus on these three areas, your lifestyle of worship will stand the test of time.

Action Point:

1.   Ask God to help you incorporate these three things into your life.

Embrace the idea of being alone with God, and actively start seeking His face.

Pray this prayer:

Dear Heavenly Father, thank You for calling me into Your dwelling place. I acknowledge that I have misunderstood the importance of being with You. Please help me to know and appreciate the value of spending time alone with You. Open my heart to embrace spiritual isolation so that I will not run from You when you call me to come away with You. Give me a desire to want You as much as You want me, and help me to acknowledge my need for a close relationship with You. I give You complete access to establish these three focuses in my life because I want to have a solid connection with You. Help me to grow in grace and in the knowledge of You so that if I fall, I'm able to get up and continue worshiping You. As You were with David, be with me, and make me a person after Your own heart. Thank You for higher heights and deeper depths in You, and may I never stop ascending into new realms of Your glory, in Jesus' name, Amen.

IV

*Corporate worship is simply an extension
of the personal worship that we give
to God when we're alone.*

Worship and the Church

"Sing to the Lord, all the earth; proclaim his salvation day after day. Declare his glory among the nations, his marvelous deeds among all peoples. For great is the Lord and most worthy of praise; he is to be feared above all gods. For all the gods of the nations are idols, but the Lord made the heavens. Splendor and majesty are before him; strength and joy in his dwelling place. Ascribe to the Lord, O families of nations, ascribe to the Lord glory and strength, ascribe to the Lord the glory due his name. Bring an offering and come before him; worship the Lord in the splendor of his holiness. Tremble before him, all the earth! The world is firmly established; it cannot be moved. Let the heavens rejoice, let the earth be glad; let them say among the nations, 'The Lord reigns!'" –I Chronicles 16:23-31 NIV

If you survey the global church, you'll discover a range of opinions about the purpose of worship; why we do it and what it is for. These differences reveal a discord that exists in our collective attitudes towards worship. As stated earlier, there are some who believe that worshiping God is either unnecessary or insignificant; while there are others who feel so uncomfortable with worship that they ignore it all together. This is why on any given Sunday you can gaze across a sanctuary and witness a mix of behaviors during the praise service; you'll see some who are passionate and fully engaged in their worship offering, some who are sitting down with disinterested looks on their faces, others who are preoccupied with their electronic devices, and those who are talking and socializing with others. In such an environment it is visibly apparent that we each regard worship with varying degrees of importance.

The practice of corporate worship is essential because it unleashes an element of God's presence and power that cannot be experienced in private worship. The church is designed to be a place infused with the presence and power of God, and as the Body of Christ, we are responsible for creating an atmosphere conducive to that objective. That is why corporate worship is so important. The worship culture of a church largely determines the spiritual atmosphere of that church. So where there is a lack of God-centered worship, there will be a lack of God's presence; and where there is a lack of God's presence, there will be a lack of God's power. A church without the presence and power of God is merely a building where people gather together to participate in religious traditions.

God is emphasizing worship and restoring its value back in the church because He wants to flood our sanctuaries with His presence and power. When the manifested presence of God is in our midst, the impact is undeniable. It turns an ordinary church service into an extraordinary service that transcends business as usual. It shifts us to another dimension in Him and empowers us with new life. With such great potential accessible to us, it's high time that we begin to acknowledge the importance of corporate worship. It's not just a song service; it's a spiritual offering that we present unto God. As we offer up worship to Him, we create an atmosphere that invites His presence to dwell in. When the church truly comes together in unity and authentically expresses worship to God, we will see a momentous outpouring of His power, and it will be a life changing experience.

"Give to the LORD the glory due His name; Bring an offering, and come into His courts. Oh, worship the LORD in the beauty of holiness..." -Psalms 96:8-9 NKJV

The structural activities of the Old Testament church teach us the importance of our worship offering. In the book of Exodus, God told Moses and the Israelites to build Him a tabernacle so that He could dwell among them. Along with that tabernacle came a set of rules on how the Israelites were to approach the presence of God. These practices are no longer in place but they provide a spiritual model for us to follow today. Inside the tabernacle was a veil that divided the room in two, the first room was the Holy Place and the second room was the Holy of Holies. Outside was a curtain that surrounded the tabernacle and enclosed the courtyard like a wall. Inside the curtain was a door, and no one could enter the courtyard without going through this door. Placed in front of this door was an altar, and each person who wanted to enter the courtyard had to enter with an animal sacrifice and put it on the altar.[1]

If you were an Israelite in those days, you would have to bring an animal with you when you went to church, and you'd have to place that animal on the altar before you could enter the sanctuary. This was not optional; if you did not bring a sacrifice you could not enter God's dwelling place. At that time, the significance of the animal sacrifice is that it was used as a payment for sin but after the atoning blood of Jesus Christ was shed (for our sins) man was no longer required to bring an animal to the altar of God. Most of us are familiar with this history, but where we falter is that we assume this protocol was completely done away with after the death and resurrection of Jesus Christ. However, that is not entirely true. In a spiritual sense, we still must follow a specific protocol when we approach the presence of God; just as the Israelites had to enter into the courtyard with an offering, we are to *"enter into his gates with thanksgiving, and into his courts*

---

[1] www.injil.org, The Tent of Meeting

with praise..." (*Psalms 100:4*).   There is still an altar in the house of God and worship is the offering that every Believer should carry with them to church.

> *"By him therefore let us offer the sacrifice of praise to God continually, that is, the fruit of our lips giving thanks to his name." -Hebrews 13:15*

From a spiritual perspective, the protocol of the animal sacrifice foreshadowed what our contemporary worship services should look like today. We are to bring our worship and place it on the altar when we enter the house of God. That is the aim of corporate worship, for the family of God to come together and honor Him with the fruit of our lips. Sadly, however, many of us go to church week after week without a sacrifice – thereby leaving the altar of God bare. This is why our corporate worship services do not garner the same measure of God's glory that the earlier church experienced.

> *"And when the trumpeters and singers were joined in unison, making one sound to be heard in praising and thanking the Lord, and when they lifted up their voice with the trumpets and cymbals and other instruments for song and praised the Lord, saying, For He is good, for His mercy and loving-kindness endure forever, then the house of the Lord was filled with a cloud, So that the priests could not stand to minister because of the cloud, for the glory of the Lord filled the house of God."*
> *-2 Chronicles 5:13-14 AMP*

When Solomon finished building the Temple of God, the people of Israel assembled themselves together for a dedication service. As the ceremony got underway, the band and the praise team began to worship God. What happened next turned out to be such a monumental display of God's glory that the Body of Christ is still talking about it today.

A casual reader may fail to notice the reason why this corporate gathering attracted God's visitation. At first glance, one might assume that God showed up simply because a building was erected in His honor, but if that were the case, manifestations such as this would occur every time a new church building is built. What actually brought God's visitation was the spirit of unity among the people in the Temple; they came together on one accord, and everyone brought an offering. God heard one heart, one voice, and one sound, and He was pleased.

As a Body of Believers, we are each individual contributors in creating a unified sound that produces one voice of worship to God. Imagine the most beautiful waltz ever heard played by the finest orchestra in the world. The dynamic which makes that waltz so beautiful is the ensemble of musicians. Each one plays their instrument in harmony with the other. And although every instrument makes its own unique sound, when you blend them together they create one magnificent song. This is an illustration of the unified sound of worship; we each have a role to play.

Can We Agree?

Agreement is a powerful principle that produces amazing results in whatever area you exercise it. The story of the Tower of Babel clearly illustrates the limitless power resident in the principle of agreement:

"Now the whole earth had one language and one speech. And it came to pass, as they journeyed from the east, that they found a plain in the land of Shinar, and they dwelt there. Then they said to one another, "Come, let us make bricks and bake them thoroughly." They had brick for stone, and they had asphalt for mortar. And they said, "Come, let us build ourselves a city, and a tower whose top is in the heavens; let us make a name for ourselves, lest we be scattered abroad over the face of the whole earth." But

the LORD came down to see the city and the tower which the sons of men had built. And the LORD said, "Indeed the people are one and they all have one language, and this is what they begin to do; now nothing that they propose to do will be withheld from them. Come, let Us go down and there confuse their language, that they may not understand one another's speech." So the LORD scattered them abroad from there over the face of all the earth, and they ceased building the city. Therefore its name is called Babel, because there the LORD confused the language of all the earth; and from there the LORD scattered them abroad over the face of all the earth."
-Genesis 11:1-9 NKJV

This was in the days of Noah when God destroyed all of the inhabitants of the earth with a Flood.   Unrighteous living was rampant and every imagination in the heart of man was full of evil intent. God looked upon the world and saw how all of humanity had corrupted its way and rebelled against His commands. "So the Lord said, 'I will wipe mankind, whom I have created, from the face of the earth — men and animals, and creatures that move along the ground, and birds of the air — for I am grieved that I have made them.' But Noah found grace in the eyes of the Lord" (Genesis 6:7-8). Noah found favor with God because he was a just and upright man. So God forewarned him of the impending flood, giving Noah and his family an opportunity to escape. In short, God provided Noah with detailed instructions to build a seaworthy vessel (otherwise known as the Ark), and bring a pair of every kind of animal (male and female) into the Ark to preserve them during the Flood. When Noah, his family, and the animals were safe onboard the Ark, floodwaters covered the earth for 150 days destroying everything on the face of the planet. Afterwards, Noah, his family, and the animals left the Ark and began repopulating the earth.

The new generation of people started advancing in technology and desired to make a name for themselves. So they collaborated with each other and devised a plan to build a monument that would commemorate their greatness – a Tower reaching all the way to the heavens. As they began building, God came down and saw the tower and He said; "Behold, they are one people and they have all one language; and this is only the beginning of what they will do, and now nothing they have imagined they can do will be impossible for them" (Genesis 11:6 AMP). The unity between the people literally made them unstoppable. God Himself said they would be able to accomplish whatever they imagined doing because they were as one. The only way to stop them from completing the tower was to sever their agreement; "Come, let Us go down and there confound (mix up, confuse) their language, that they may not understand one another's speech. So the Lord scattered them abroad from that place upon the face of the whole earth, and they gave up building the city" (Genesis 11:7-8 AMP).

Unity generates power and it attracts God's attention; that's why it's one of the most vital components of a worship service. Furthermore, and perhaps most important, unity attracts God's attention because it is the quintessential expression of His son Jesus Christ. As Christians, God has grafted us into the body of Christ (I Corinthians 12:12-13), this means, though we are many individuals, we have been made as one *in* Christ Jesus. Just as there is no division inside a natural body, there should be no division inside the spiritual body of Christ. When God looks at the church, He is looking for the personification of His son; and the moment He sees unity expressed through us, we get His undivided attention. When the principle of unity begins to fully operate in our worship services, the outcome will be supernatural.

In theory, we understand the concept of unity, but as a whole, our challenge lies in carrying it out. If the spirit of unity were fully functioning in our worship services, everyone – from the youngest to the oldest, the pastors, the deacons, the ushers, the ministers and the laymen; whether in the front of the church, the back of the church or in the balcony – would bring an offering into the house of the Lord.   But when we observe our services we do not see the unity.   We see some who come with an offering and others who do not.

> *"May the God who gives endurance and encouragement give you a spirit of unity among yourselves as you follow Christ Jesus, so that with one heart and mouth you may glorify the God and Father of our Lord Jesus Christ."*
> *–Romans 15:5-6 NIV*

Unity is defined as a state or condition of perfect harmony; oneness of mind *and* feeling among a group of people.   In the context of corporate worship, full-scale participation is one element of unity, but an equally important aspect of unity lies in the participants hearts and minds.   Do we share the same mindset and heart attitude about worshiping God or do we just go through the motions when we come together to worship?   When we worship, our minds should be focused solely on God. We should not be thinking about our issues, our to-do lists or where we're planning to go after church; our minds should be totally engrossed and completely engaged in what we're offering to God. Likewise, when we worship, our heart's desire should be for the presence of God and nothing else. We should not have a list of desires (in our heart) that we want God to fulfill in exchange for our worship, (this applies to personal worship also). We should have hearts that desires God's presence more than anything else.

The condition of our heart towards each other is also very critical. As Christians, we should not have any strife or dissension between us (I Peter 1:22 & I Corinthians 3:3); we should love one another with pure hearts.   Nothing jeopardizes unity more than strife and offense. When we harbor offense in our heart towards another, it creates division in the Body and pollutes our worship offering. For this reason, it is imperative that we quickly forgive and work diligently to resolve conflicts when they arise. This is all a part of the perfect harmony that should be resident in our services.

Preparation is Key

It is fair to say that many churches are filled with indifference towards worshiping God. In today's culture we feel free to do as we please, so we come to church with a lackadaisical attitude and allow our mode to determine whether we're going to worship God or not. We typically go to church with an expectation to receive (from God), but rarely anticipate what we're going to give (to God), and so, we're generally ill-prepared to worship. If this were still the era of animal sacrifices, you would have to prepare an offering beforehand, you wouldn't be able to carelessly fall out of bed, get dressed and go to the tabernacle. If you did not prepare your sacrifice ahead of time, you would have nothing to bring to the altar, and thereby be excluded from entering the presence of God. Yet, in today's environment, many of us don't even arrive on time for the worship service. We trickle in late, distracted, disconnected from the atmosphere, and ultimately ignore the altar of God.

In order for our collective expression of worship to reach its full potential, we must prepare our offering prior to the service. First and foremost, you cannot be a worshiper in public if you're not a worshiper in private. This is perhaps the reason why so many of us struggle in a corporate setting, because we don't have a private relationship with God. Worship is intimacy, and true intimacy is expressed one-on-one behind closed doors. It's easy to show affection for God in *public* if you've been intimate with Him in *private*, but if you haven't spent time with Him alone then corporate worship will feel very awkward to you. Corporate worship is simply an extension of the personal worship that we give to God when we're alone. This is why it's important for every Christian to have an active relationship with God, and spend regular time worshiping Him in private. Those who do not minister to God in private have very little to offer Him in a corporate setting, and that undermines the spirit of unity that the church is striving to achieve.

To meet with God we should prepare for worship at least a day before church. For example, take the time to consciously wind down and quiet your mind. In that place of stillness, put your focus on God and prayerfully consider the quality of offering you want to bring to the altar. Pray for the Holy Spirit to help you bring an offering that is fit for the King. Pray that your mind will be attentive during worship and that your motive will be to encounter God's presence and nothing else. Pray for those in attendance to be on one accord. Pray that God is exalted through every aspect of the service. Pray for the musicians and worship singers to effectively minister under the anointing of God. Lastly, if you're facing any challenges, take this time to give those challenges over to God. Let them go and trust God with them. Remember how He delivered you out of your last challenge, and know that He's going to be just as faithful to you this time around.

If you're going through a difficult time, this will be an especially helpful exercise. Quite often, when we're stressed or in the midst of a trial, we let the weight of our challenges bury our faith and consume us with worry and fear. We fixate on our problems and lose sight of the goodness of God. If we don't consciously lay our challenges aside, we will inevitably carry them with us to church and we won't be free to worship. Our minds will be riddled with anxiety and we'll be incapable of focusing on God.

> *"Casting the whole of your care [all your anxieties, all your worries, all your concerns, once and for all] on Him, for He cares for you affectionately and cares about you watchfully." –I Peter 5:7 AMP*

God has already given us a remedy for the challenges we face. We are to give them over to Him. I remember when I was a child and encountered problems that I could not resolve on my own; whether I skinned my knee, required help tying my shoelaces or lacked the strength necessary to open a bottle of juice. I automatically knew that if I gave the problem over to one of my parents, they would fix it for me. And they always did. As a result, I lived a relatively carefree life when I was a kid, because I did not bear the responsibility of fixing my own problems. My parents fixed all of them for me. Similarly, our heavenly Father desires for us to have the same type of relationship with Him. He wants us to confidently cast our cares on Him, and trust that He will fix them for us. It may sound overly simple, but it's true. God does not want us to be burdened and heavy laden with the challenges of life. He wants to sustain us and cause us to triumph over all that we go through.

If we allow our challenges to prevent us from worshiping God, we rob ourselves of the very thing we need to make it through the hard places in life. Primarily, we need two things when we're going through a difficult season; strength and wisdom. We need strength to make it through to the end, and wisdom to know what to do to win. Strength, along with a host of other great things, is found in the presence of the Lord, (I Chronicles 16:27). That is why, when we allow our circumstances to stop our worship, we unwittingly delay ourselves from receiving what we need the most.

> *"Exalt the LORD our God, and worship at his holy hill; for the LORD our God is holy." -Psalms 99:9*

Unfortunately, this scenario plays itself out week after week, all over the Body of Christ. Christians go to church so burdened by their problems, they can't even worship God. What we fail to realize is, when we allow our problems to stop us from worshiping God, we exalt them above God. When we exalt our problems above God, we make them bigger than He is, in our eyes. Anything that is bigger than God inevitably has the power to defeat us. So whenever we make our challenges bigger than God, we solidify our own failure. This is why it's so important to worship God in the face of all that we go through, because worship magnifies God. When we magnify God above our problems, we give Him access to move in them, and that is the key to our victory. Therefore, it behooves all of us to prepare ourselves for worship, so that when we get to church we're able to rightly exalt the one true living God.

Another aspect of preparation involves very practical steps. For example, we should tend to the things that will cause us to arrive late for church, if left undone until the last minute. Such as, fuel up your car the night before, prepare the attire you plan to wear, and get a good night's rest to ensure you wake up in a timely manner. Finally, you should leave for church early enough to arrive at least 10 minutes before the service starts. These things may seem small, but if we put them into practice, we will see a huge difference in our worship services.

> *"I was glad when they said unto me, Let us go into the house of the LORD." -Psalms 122:1*

We should go to church with a lavish offering for God, one filled with passion, adoration and praise; and we should appreciate the value of church. The Church, among other things, is a safe haven for Believers, a place where we can meet with God and soak in His wonderful presence. It is where our spirits are fed and our strength is renewed. We can fellowship with people of like-faith, encourage one another and receive transformative revelation from the preaching of the Word. Knowing these great benefits await us at church, we should eagerly bring our best offering into the house of God.

To Sing or Not to Sing

> *"Sing unto the LORD, O ye saints of his, and give thanks at the remembrance of his holiness." -Psalms 30:4*

Corporate worship is participatory, meaning, it requires more than just observation on our part. In a church filled with people, opposite a platform with musicians and worship singers, it's easy to become a spectator of the proceedings and not actually engage in the act of worship. It's also easy to mistake the worship team for musical performers who are putting on a show for our benefit. However, this is not what corporate worship is about. Corporate worship is solely for God's benefit, and the worship team is not there to sing *to* us or to perform *for* us, their function is to encourage us and lead us to communicate our own worship to God. So often we're content just listening to the worship team sing, as opposed to worshiping along with them - especially if the people around us aren't worshiping either. But as we mature into true worshipers, we realize that no one can worship God for us, and by not participating, we're missing out on the blessings of corporate worship.

> *"O bless our God, ye people, and make the voice of his praise to be heard..." -Psalms 66:8*

As previously stated, the corporate voice of worship is incomplete without full participation, because each individual voice blends together to form one sound. In a sea of people lifting their voices up to God, He hears you specifically, and something is missing in His ears when you choose to keep silent. We are called to make God's praises heard, so we cannot just worship Him in our hearts or rely on others to worship Him for us, we have to lift up our own voices and bless God with the fruit of our lips. An interesting thing happens during corporate worship; the actions of one person can impact the actions of others and create a ripple effect that spreads throughout the service. You can influence others with your worship, or lack thereof. When people – who either do not feel like worshiping, do not know how to worship, or feel uncomfortable worshiping – observe your worship, many times they will feel convicted or inspired to follow suit. As they begin worshiping, they can impact those around them in the same manner. Similarly, when you keep silent, the effect on the service is more or less the same. When you choose not to worship, you can potentially dissuade those around you from worshiping also.

If you choose to worship, then your worship must be intentional, not just something you fall into if the conditions are right. Oftentimes we go to church, and if the worship team does not sing our favorite song, or if the band doesn't sound 'just right', we disengage and refuse to worship. This type of behavior promotes disunity and is indicative of superficiality. When we allow our attitudes and proclivities to dictate our worship, our worship becomes superficial and self-centered. Self-centered worship is an affront to God and hinders the release of His presence. If God is not the center of our worship, then what are we worshiping for?

Things won't always be perfect in a church service, but perfection is not the goal. Yes, we should do our best to execute our services with a spirit of excellence, but if we miss the mark, it shouldn't derail the entire service. Understand that God is not drawn by the aesthetics of our worship; He's drawn by our passion for Him. So if the keyboardist plays the wrong note, or if the choir sounds a little off key, we should move beyond those production flaws and turn our affections toward God. Realize, what may sound bad to your ears is music to God's ears if the motive of the worshiper is pure. Thus, we must never lose sight of what true worship is all about; it's not about good music or good singing. True worship is about honoring God and glorifying Him with a pure heart. That is the reason why we worship.

The Body of Christ is experiencing a global shift in the way we view worship, individually and corporately. God Himself is spearheading this shift and each of us must decide whether to embrace it or reject it. Embracing this shift requires us to put aside our old approach to worship - which at times has been uninspired and insincere - and move to a more purposeful passionate approach, one which has God's heart at the forefront.

Worship is very important to God so it should be very important to the church. If we understand that God designed worship to be a means for us to demonstrate our love to Him, then we should willingly join together and collectively participate in this act. When the Body of Christ genuinely comes together as one, with hearts that hunger for God and desire to please Him, we will experience a level of glory that will far surpass what the earlier church experienced.

Summary

God is preparing to visit His church and worship is setting the stage for His visitation. Now more than ever, we must intentionally bring an offering into the house of God, and we must each take responsibility for the role we play in the corporate expression of worship. If we embrace the call of the hour, we will experience the glory of God at a magnitude so great, the impact will be undeniable.

Action Point:

1.   Ask God to show you where you fall short, in the area of corporate worship.

Let God reveal to you His vision for corporate worship, and then allow Him to work through you to bring that vision to pass. Be willing to relinquish old methods of doing things in exchange for new ways that may take you outside of your comfort zone.

Pray this prayer:

Dear Heavenly Father, thank You for the habitation of Your house, the place where Your glory dwells. I am grateful for the opportunity to assemble with other Believers and exalt You in the Tabernacle. I acknowledge that I have not always brought an offering to the altar, but I'm willing to change and do things Your way. Forgive me for the times when I devalued the importance of worship and withheld it from You. Help me to respect Your desire for worship and to view it from Your perspective from this point forward. Give me the unction to minister to You in private so that I'm comfortable demonstrating my affection for You in public. Help me not to be ashamed to worship You in front of others, and remind me that You are my audience of one. I pray for unity to increase in the Body of Christ so that we may see Your glory such as never before. Thank you for what You are about to do in the midst of Your people, in Jesus name, Amen!

V

Too many Christians live on the outskirts of God's glory, admiring Him from a distance but never encountering Him up close and personal.

The Worshiper in You

"Blessed are those you choose and bring near to live in your courts! We are filled with the good things of your house, of your holy temple." —Psalms 65:4 NIV

I grew up in a godly household; as a child, I had to memorize bible verses and abide by a strict code of conduct. Our family went to church every week and we held bible study meetings in our home. I sang in the choir and participated in every church activity for my age group. I honestly do not remember a time in my childhood when God was not emphasized in one form or another. Yet, throughout my upbringing and early adult life I never knew, nor was I taught, that God desired to have a personal relationship with me. No one ever presented that to me as an option or a concept. The absence of this knowledge led me to develop a performance-based mentality with God; meaning, I thought my value to Him was tied to how well I performed. I felt that God would only love me if I did everything that a good little Christian girl should do. Whenever I fell short of where I thought I should be, I felt condemned and thrown away by God. I viewed Him as a far off distant being that set impossible standards for me to follow. God was nothing more to me than an abstract idea, someone I knew of religiously but not relationally.

Devoid of a personal connection with God, I never experienced His love. Intellectually, I believed that God loved me but I wasn't assured of it in my heart. Over the years I became very skillful at presenting the perfect Christian façade, I exuded confidence in God's love for me and I encouraged others to be confident in His love for them. Inwardly, however, I felt dispassionate and indifferent towards God because I didn't know Him. Furthermore, I did not truly believe that God cared for people at a personal level. I felt that we were all just subjects made to fall in line and do whatever He said to do. For me, Christianity had nothing to do with God's love; it was all about conformity and behavior modification.

It would be 23 years into my Christian faith before I'd learn about the concept of intimacy with God. Admittedly, during those years I became very misguided by my religious convictions. I grew into a spiritual snob, someone who was very overbearing to be around. I argued about the Bible with people who didn't see things my way, I looked down on others who didn't live their lives the same as I did, and I felt superior to those who didn't believe in Jesus Christ. I was dogmatic, self-righteousness and judgmental, completely ignorant to the fact that I was not displaying God's true character. In retrospect, it would have been impossible for me to display God's character because I did not know Him. It was only after I began to seek God, by spending time with Him that I learned about His true nature. (Note: If your belief system does not cause or inspire you to display God's character, you should question the source of your convictions).

After years of being a misguided Christian, I soon felt led to leave my hometown and start fresh somewhere else. I relocated to a new state and began attending a non-denominational spirit-filled church. It was there that I was introduced to the concept of intimacy with God. In the months and years that followed, I developed a personal relationship with God and began hearing His voice for the first time in my life. Following His voice set me on a path that transformed my life and changed my entire belief system. I discovered that God is nothing like I thought He was; He is not critical or mean, and He doesn't turn His back on people who choose not to believe in Him. He is not an angry King sitting on His throne waiting to condemn mankind for all of our misdeeds. He is merciful and compassionate, and His love is sweeter than anything you could ever imagine.

There's no greater love than the love of God; it's boundless, eternal and relentless. It's able to soften callous hearts, heal wounded emotions and illuminate the darkest soul. It embraces the outcast and frees the guilty from sin. It's a safe place to fall and a force that enables you to rise to heights unimaginable. There is nothing like the love of God.

God is love and His love is experienced in the confines of relationship. If we don't have a relationship with God we go through life with a love deficit. A love deficit is a critical condition that if left untreated will chip away at your spiritual health and vitality. To understand the impact of a love deficit, we can look at the early developmental stage of an infant. Research shows that babies need touch and emotional engagement in order to grow and develop. Babies who are not held and hugged enough will literally stop growing and, if the situation lasts long enough, die. The ones who survive become high risk for behavioral, emotional, and social problems as they grow up.[1] This is the spiritual phenomenon that takes place in us when a love deficit occurs. The impact may not result in a natural death, but the effects are substantial nonetheless. From the moment we are born, our deepest and most profound need is to be loved. This need is utterly fulfilled when we become intimate with God. That is why the importance of developing a relationship with God can never be

---

[1] Maia Szalvitz, Touching Empathy (Psychology Today blog, posted Mar 01, 2010)

understated, it is the most important relationship we can have. If we don't take the time to build a relationship with God, we will never fully experience love.

I presume many of us are living with a love deficit but we either fail to recognize it or have become so accustomed to it that we've accepted the deficit as a normal part of life. Some of the more obvious signs of a love deficit are: 1) a general sense of feeling unloved, 2) an inability to communicate love to those you're closest with, 3) a pervasive feeling of emptiness. These issues are indicative of a deficit and they leave us feeling weak, hopeless and alone. Sadly, most of us don't know how to address our issues so we fill our lives with meaningless activity or anesthetize ourselves with different vices to alleviate the pain we carry around inside. The truth is, God's love is the only remedy for a love deficit, but we must take the time to build a relationship with Him to receive the love we so desperately need.

So What's the Problem?

The biggest challenge I faced in building a relationship with God stemmed from a flawed concept I had about Christianity. Growing up I belonged to a religious denomination which taught very structured beliefs and practices. These teachings led me to believe that Christians were made right with God by following man-made rules and doing good deeds. This way of thinking became the lens that I viewed my Christian faith through. As a result, I thought the sum total of Christianity was: go to church, read the bible and obey the "rules." I did not know there was more, and because I did not know there was more I was content *practicing* religion without actually *knowing* the God of my religion. Many of us think we have a relationship with God simply because we're members of a denomination and perform religious activities, but that's not true. Religion can give you information about God but it cannot give you a relationship with God. Only you can develop a relationship with God for yourself. This is not to say that information about God is unimportant or irrelevant, on the contrary, we need information about God to establish a basis for our faith. However, we cannot stop there; we must seek to know Him on a personal level. The problem is that many of us know *about* God but don't actually *know* God. This is why relationship is so vitally important, because it gives you a living experience with God. Unless you have a living experience with God you will not know Him.

Let me interject this point to clarify the statement I made about religion. I'm not bashing religion or religious denominations, I am saying that regardless of our religious affiliation, God wants His children to know Him and not just know *about* Him. Whether Baptist, Catholic, Adventist, Presbyterian, etc...the commonality that all Christians share is that we each must seek to know God for ourselves.

Our highest priority in life should be to know God. Paul, one of the most prolific apostles of the New Testament era, penned an insightful scripture about what it takes to know the Lord:

> "...*If any other man considers that he has reason to rely on the flesh and his physical and outward advantages, I have more! Circumcised when I was eight days old, of the race of Israel, of the tribe of Benjamin, a Hebrew of Hebrews; as to the observance of the Law I was of the Pharisees, As to my zeal, I was a persecutor of the church, and by the Law's standard of righteousness I was proven to be blameless and no fault was found with me. But whatever former things I had that might have been gains to me, I have come to consider as loss for Christ's sake. Yes, furthermore, I count everything as loss compared to the possession of the priceless privilege of knowing Christ Jesus my Lord and of progressively becoming more deeply and intimately acquainted with Him.*"
> –*Philippians 3:4-8 AMP*

Paul's passion was to know Jesus and he prioritized his life accordingly. In essence, he took all of his accomplishments, his pedigree, and his desires and put them on the backburner to focus on the "priceless privilege" of knowing the Lord. Our life's passion should mirror that of Paul's–to become deeply and intimately acquainted with God. Becoming intimate with God is a precious opportunity that is available to everyone, but few people take advantage of it because the cost is high. I have struggled greatly with paying the price, I've been inconsistent with God, I've faltered and I've even felt like knowing Him was not worth the effort. But when I truly set everything else aside in exchange for seeking Him, I stepped into a love that is unparalleled to anything I've experienced in life.

In order to know God, we have to make Him a priority in our lives and spend time studying His Word. The Bible is the master key to knowing God because it is God's revelation of Himself to man. By studying the Word, we're able to learn *who* God is, *how* He relates to us and what He desires *from* us. It is impossible to know God without knowing His Word.

Another level of *knowing* God involves being intimate with Him. Being intimate with God means to enter His presence naked and unashamed–completely stripped of any pretenses. As we stand before Him, we must let down all of our defenses and allow Him to see everything – including the things about ourselves that we don't like. God already knows everything there is to know about us, and He loves us unconditionally, but if we aren't fully transparent with Him, we will never truly believe that He loves us in spite of our faults.

Intimacy with God cannot be achieved without having a relationship with God. Some people shy away from pursuing a relationship with God because they don't know where to start. But developing a relationship with God is not complicated; you can genuinely establish a bond with Him similar to the way your personal relationships are formed. If, for example, you want to demonstrate love and build an intimate relationship with someone, you first need to know what that person wants and likes. Then, you would spend quality time with that person doing the things that they want and like. The same is true with God.   If you're going to establish a real connection with Him, you need to spend quality time with Him doing the things that He wants and likes. As previously stated, the Bible teaches that God *wants* and *likes* worship (see John 4:23 and Revelation 5:11-12), therefore, the best way to begin building a relationship with God is to spend quality time worshiping Him.

The Journey Begins

Shortly after relocating to a new state, I moved into my own place. This was a first for me, because prior to this, I either lived with my parents or had a roommate. On the day that I moved-in I immediately sensed that God did not want me to connect my TV or hook up any of my electronic devices. At that moment, I instantly knew that God and I were about to take a journey together, and I sensed that something new and different was getting ready to happen in my life. I had no idea what was about to transpire, but I knew God was orchestrated things, so I was excited about what was to come.

After a couple of weeks, I unpacked all of my boxes and was finally able to enjoy my new surroundings. The only thing missing was the familiar sound of a television set playing in the background. Of course I questioned whether God truly told me not to connect my TV, but every time I was tempted to turn it on, I felt convicted not to, so I let it go.

One morning, as I was going about my normal routine, I walked into my living room and out of the blue I felt a strong urge to worship God. So I put on a worship CD and began singing to the Lord. This was definitely not normal for me; I sang in the church choir as a little girl and always participated in corporate worship services, but I never sang to the Lord in private before. At this point, intimacy with God was a developing concept, but I hadn't actually experienced it yet.

As I sang along with the worship CD a ton of feelings came over me. I felt awkward, uncomfortable, apprehensive, and even a little embarrassed. I was completely unsure about what I was doing and I didn't fully know why I was doing it. I didn't like the sound of my voice, I thought about what my neighbors would think if they heard me, and I even thought it was impossible for my singing to touch God. Yet, in the midst of all those feelings, I knew that my journey with the Lord had just begun.

For the next couple of weeks I made sure to spend at least 30 minutes a day worshiping God. As time passed, I became more comfortable and less apprehensive about singing out loud; the awkwardness started to fade and I began to look forward to our time together.

"But I will sing of your strength; I will sing aloud of your steadfast love in the morning..." -Psalms 59:16 NKJV

One morning as I prepared for worship I put in a music CD, but instead of pressing play, I spontaneously began singing my own song to God. I sang about my devotion for Him and my appreciation for His faithfulness in my life. While I was singing, many of God's attributes came to mind so I introduced them into the song as well. My spirit became engaged at a level it had not been before. Instead of using someone else's lyrics to express my feelings for God, I pulled the words out of my own heart with intent and passion. This was the moment that changed everything for me; this was the moment when my worship became personal. It was no longer a concept or an activity, but it was me becoming intimate with God. In that moment, I realized that I had a direct line to God's heart.

I developed such a passion for worship and I had

encounters with God that I cannot put into words. The very first time I experienced His presence I didn't even know what it was, but I knew something amazing was happening. The entire atmosphere changed and I felt something moving inside of me. Tears began to flow and I scurried around my mind in search of the perfect song to sing. But I was rendered speechless by the presence of God. He was nearer than I'd ever experienced Him before. Nothing else mattered. All I wanted was to hold on to that moment for as long as I possibly could. The moment didn't last, but inwardly I knew that I had been touched by God and that a significant shift had just occurred.

As I grew in worship, so many things changed in my life. I experienced new levels of peace and became acutely aware that God was with me, in me and for me. There were days when it felt like God had laid out a red carpet before me and lined my path with nothing but favor. I didn't have to struggle and strive to get things. When challenges came, I worshiped through them and was able to triumph over things that beforehand would have crushed the life out of me.

I even discovered my worth in worship. Prior to encountering God's presence, I saw myself as an outcast, someone who was picked over and left to the side. This insecurity developed in my childhood as a result of certain experiences that I went through. Particularly, in grade school when teams were selected for sports games, one by one I watched as all of my classmates were picked to be on a team, but my name was never called. I had to be placed on a team by default. While I could not articulate it at the time, these types of experiences made me feel fundamentally unwanted. One morning in worship, I heard the spirit of God say to me: "I did not pass over you; I picked you and placed you on the winning team." I was blown away! I realized that God had always wanted me and He waited patiently for me to come to the place of worship so that we could commune together. This was it for me; I had found the love of my life, someone who loved me without reservations or conditions. Someone who saw value in me and wasn't ashamed to be associated with me just because I didn't look a certain way.

Morning after morning I'd worship and soak in God's presence. Some mornings were different than others, there were times when His presence was so pronounced it was palpable, and then there were times when it felt as if He hid Himself from me so that I could seek Him in a deeper way. There were even times when He did the unexpected and left me completely amazed. One such time was May 18, 2004, a day that I will never forget. Two years prior I heard a teaching about the Baptism of the Holy Spirit with the evidence of speaking in tongues (Mark 16:17, I Corinthians 14:5). At the time, I did not believe that speaking in tongues was of God because I had been taught that it was unbiblical. However, this teaching was so in-depth and compelling, I went home that evening and asked God to show me whether it was legitimate or not. In the weeks that followed, I did extensive research on the subject and prayed for God to reveal the truth to me. Not long after, as a result of researching the Word, I became convinced that speaking in tongues was a gift from God. At the precise moment when I came to this realization, I received a phone call from one of my girlfriends. To my surprise, my girlfriend confessed that she felt led to send me a book which explained the gift of speaking in tongues, (The Holy Spirit, by Frederick K.C. Price, Ph.D.), but she never followed through with it because she knew that I didn't believe in speaking in tongues. I explained to her all that had transpired and how I was seeking God for the truth about the Baptism of the Holy Spirit. She realized that she heard God correctly and should have sent me the book when He told her to.

When I finally received the book, it served as a source of confirmation and further convinced me that speaking in tongues was a gift from God. So I prayed and asked for the Baptism of the Holy Spirit. Almost two years went by and nothing happened. After a while I stopped praying about it and resolved that maybe it just wasn't for me. I still believed my new found understanding of tongues, but I started to feel that it was only for certain people and not the masses. Soon, my desire faded to the background and only resurfaced when I was in the presence of someone who spoke in tongues.

Tuesday, May 18th, began as an average day. I woke up and started my normal routine completely unaware that I was moments away from an encounter with God. At 12:03 PM, I entered my quiet place and began worshiping the Lord. I sang two songs and on the third song the power of God fell upon me and I felt electricity surge throughout my entire body. I dropped to my knees and wept. Suddenly, tongues began swirling around in my head and all I had to do was open up my mouth and release them. There I was in the middle of my room speaking in tongues and worshiping God. This continued for almost two hours and then I felt praise welling up inside of me. I knew this praise was going to be pretty intense, so when it reached a point where I could no longer contain it, I put my face into a pillow and released the loudest shout of hallelujah, over and over and over again. It was the most incredible experience. I was completely awe-struck for days afterward and found it very difficult to go back to my normal life.

The more I grew in worship, the more anchored I became in God, and whenever I drifted away from Him, His love always pulled me back to our secret place.

I have discovered that apart from God my strength dwindles, my hopes fade and I'm one step away from giving up. But when I focus on Him and remain steadfast in worship, I have unshakeable peace and faith to stand even in the midst of extreme adversity.

Worship changes you; when you come face-to-face with the presence of God, nothing stays the same. It's an encounter of seismic proportions that shifts everything inside you. No longer will you be satisfied with just a Sunday morning experience with

God, your heart will cry for more. One moment in God's presence revolutionizes your entire concept of Him and creates a desire within you to know Him in a deeper way. Too many Christians live on the outskirts of God's glory, admiring Him from a distance but never encountering Him up close and personal. Worship connects you to the heart of God and ushers you into the place where His glory dwells.

You are a worshiper. You may not identify as such, but you are a worshiper. You may have never experienced a worship encounter with God, but you are a worshiper. Worship is a part of your spiritual DNA whether you recognize it or not. Many Christians do not even realize it, but every Believer has a ministry of worship to God, it is a part of our life's purpose.

> *"But you are a chosen people, a royal priesthood, a holy nation, a people belonging to God, that you may declare the praises of him who called you out of darkness into his wonderful light." -I Peter 2:0 NIV*

As stated in Chapter 3, the Priests were specifically chosen by God to minister unto Him in the Temple (see Deuteronomy 10:8). Among other things, the Priests were God's personal worshipers, an elite group of men who had exclusive access into His presence (which was kept behind a veil in the Temple). When Jesus died on the cross as a sacrifice for our sins, the veil in the temple was torn in two from top to bottom. This signified that the way into God's presence was now open to anyone who would accept Jesus as their personal savior. So when the Bible refers to New Testament Christians as a "royal priesthood," in part, this means that we are God's personal worshipers, a group of people specifically chosen to come into His presence and minister unto Him. This is who you are!

You may feel as if there are things in your past that disqualify you from worshiping God, but that is not true. The enemy loves to try and convince us that we're not good enough to worship God or that we're not worthy to enter His presence. The truth is, our access to God's presence is not based on our own righteousness, it's based on the righteousness of Christ. Jesus' blood paid the price for all of our sins and it is the basis whereby God accepts our worship (provided that we repent from all known sin). When we repent from sin, God blots out our transgressions and remembers them no more (Isaiah 43:25). So when we come before God, He does not have a checklist of all our wrongdoings, He has arms open wide eager to welcome us into His throne room. This is why we can worship God with boldness and confidence, and never fear that we're unwelcome in His presence. Whenever the enemy tries to remind you of your past, remind him of the blood and cast his thoughts out of your mind.

The Journey Continues

A worship relationship with God is a journey that once embarked upon will take you from one level of glory to the next. When you worship, God will reveal different facets of Himself as you progress in your quest for more of Him. In many ways, the journey should always challenge you to keep moving forward with God. You should never get to a place of familiarity and choose to stop advancing.

On this journey, you'll have to resist the temptation to reduce worship into a routine or try to craft a formula for it. Routines are counterproductive and can cause you to hit a worship plateau. If that happens, you will stop moving forward and cease growing as a worshiper. Formulas and routines are oftentimes put into practice to make things convenient for people and to control the outcome of worship. But worship cannot be controlled or manipulated by man's efforts – regardless of how noble those efforts may be. Worship can only be driven by a fresh desire for God's glory. If we do not hunger for God, we will not experience the fullness of His presence. The reason why many of us tend to prefer formulas is because they're predictable and easy. But, if we utilize a formula for worship, we will not be engaged at the level we need to be in order to stir our passion for the presence of God.

I remember when I first encountered God's presence; I wanted all of my succeeding worship experiences to mirror that one encounter.   So from then on, I approached worship in the exact same way and expected the exact same results.   Sometimes God did what I expected Him to, but other times, He did not. This left me feeling slightly confused. After a season of what felt like playing cat and mouse with God, I realized that I had created my own frustration.   I was trying to build my entire worship experience around that one encounter, but God wanted to take me to another place in Him. He wanted to reveal a facet of Himself that I had yet to discover, but I thought that I had already experienced the be-all and end-all of God so I was satisfied and wanted to remain in the place where I was.

When we chase after a specific experience in worship, we pigeonhole God from disclosing more of Himself to us. For this reason, it is important that we give God the freedom to design our journey however He sees fit, and then relinquish control so that He can lead us wherever He desires.   The key is that we must continually approach worship with fresh expectation and a resolve to chase after God and not after an experience.

Whenever God reveals a new dimension of Himself, it always comes with an invitation to go deeper. Going deeper simply means to increase the intensity of our passion so that we can move to the next place in God. Remember, there are endless realms and countless dimensions in God, so we will never get to a place where we've experienced all there is to experience in Him; there will always be more. This is why we must continue to move forward in worship, because if we attempt to remain in the place of our last discovery, we will eventually get bored and become stagnant in our relationship with God.

Weeds, Weeds and More Weeds!

Building a relationship with God is much like cultivating a garden. There's a lot more to gardening than just planting and harvesting. You don't just plant seeds, go on your merry way and come back in a few weeks to begin harvesting a crop. You have to pay attention to your garden every step of the way if you want to grow a premium bountiful crop. Cultivating, in part, is the process of removing weeds from a garden. Weeds are undesirable plants that grow where they are not wanted. They are invasive and rob plants of resources needed for growth, including nutrients, water, and sunlight. Weeds also host pathogens that can infect a garden with vegetative diseases. If left uncontrolled, weeds will reduce yields and lower the quality of your crop. There is no way to permanently eliminate weeds without killing your garden, but the process of cultivating will help to minimize weed growth.

When you plant a garden, you have to be vigilant and inspect it on a regular basis. The moment you detect early signs of weeds, it's time to take action. Weeds spring up quickly and seemingly grow overnight, if you don't deal with them early on they will spread and overtake your garden.

Establishing a relationship with God is one thing, cultivating it is another. In order to preserve the presence of God in your life, you have to guard against those things that can potentially ruin your relationship. Just like gardening, you have to keep the weeds out. Weeds are those things that undermine your relationship and threaten its stability. If you don't keep the weeds out, your relationship won't stand the test of time. You must realize that a relationship with God is not self-sustaining; it won't take care of itself nor will it flourish on its own. You have to tend your garden if you want longevity with God. The constancy of your connection is solely determined by you, therefore, you have to decide what you want; do you want His presence to rest in your life, or will you be satisfied with just a touch of Him here and there. In my own journey I've experienced both ends of the spectrum; I've had seasons where it felt like my life was enveloped in the presence of God, and then there were seasons when I neglected my garden and created a void between God and I. Those times taught me how precious God's presence is; it's the one thing in life that I cannot live without.

The interesting fact about weeds is that all of them are not pesky looking wild plants; some of them actually look like flowers. This tells us that we cannot take things at face value when it concerns our relationship with God. We must examine everything that comes within close proximity of our garden, because some things may look good but are actually weeds in disguise. All weeds are opportunistic and harmful to the health of your garden, so you must be watchful and prepared to deal with them at a moment's notice. I've observed three types of weeds that will destroy your relationship if left uncontrolled. Let's examine each one carefully so that we have a clear picture of the challenges we'll face in cultivating our garden with God.

✟   **Distractions-** Distractions are those things that divert your attention and draw you away from the task at hand. They hinder your focus and cause you to lose sight of your goals. Distractions are the most insidious weeds because they spring up everywhere and continually threaten to take you off track. They constantly war for your attention and never go away. We live in a world of distractions; never is this more apparent than when you set out to accomplish a goal. Things that weren't problematic before now demand your attention and seek to consume all of your time. If you don't learn to effectively manage distractions you will be unable to nurture and maintain your relationship with God.

When it comes to your relationship with God, time is your most precious commodity. Time is one of the few things in life that you cannot get back once it's spent. We all have a finite amount of time to accomplish whatever we want to accomplish with our lives; when our time expires we'll no longer have the opportunity to do the things we'd hope to have done. For this reason, it behooves each of us to live attentively and manage our time wisely.

To be wise stewards of our time, we must first define what we want from life by identifying the things that matter most to us. Next, we need to develop goals that will help move us in the direction of our desires. Then, once we determine what our goals are we have to set aside time to carry them out. Every day we should spend time doing something to advance our goals.

How you spend your time reveals what's most valuable to you. You can say your relationship with God is important, but if you don't set aside regular time to spend with Him your actions reveal a dichotomy. The truth is many of us spend very little time doing things that support our goals. As a result, there's a mismatch between what we say we desire and what we actually have. You cannot *have* a flourishing relationship with God if you do not spend time with Him on a regular basis. If someone really matters to you, you make time for them no matter what. You don't put them off or make up excuses as to why you can't spend time with them.

As Believers, we must have an active relationship with God to stay connected to our faith and live victorious lives. We need His presence more than anything because He is the source of life and apart from Him we're spiritually dead. Show me a person who is not actively pursuing or nurturing a relationship with God and I'll show you a person who is tired, at their wits end and defeated by the challenges of life. Every attempt to live independently from God results in unpleasant consequences; this is evident in the number of people who live broken and unfulfilled lives. Only when we walk closely with God do we discover lasting joy, sustainable peace and a sense of purpose in life. Realizing our need for God should motivate us to make Him a priority in our lives. If we make God a priority, then our primary goal must be a lifetime commitment to build and sustain a relationship with Him. We have to resolve to give as much attention to our relationship with God as we do to the relationships that mean the most to us in life, such as our relationship with our spouse, our children, etc...

We each must create spaces in our lives that are reserved exclusively for God; a time and place where we go to be alone with Him on a regular basis. The time can be whenever you chose, early in the morning, late at night or anything in between- just decide what works best for you and then stick to it. The place can also be your choice; a bedroom, basement, closet, living room or even a car, just be sure to select a location that will give you the most amount of privacy. Once you designate a place and time, and commit to spending regular time with God, you will have to guard that time with extreme sobriety because distractions will come, and if you aren't careful they will impede your commitment.

For those of us who've lived any length of time, we know from experience that life has a way of getting out of control; problems can arise out of nowhere and things can change in the blink of an eye. The car breaks down and disrupts your normal routine. Family members get sick and need your help. A pressing deadline on the job suddenly requires you to work extra hours. The list goes on and on; there's no limit to the amount of things life can throw at us on a frequent basis. For this reason, we must develop laser sharp focus on our priorities, if not, before we know it a year goes by and we've failed at our commitment to spend regular time with God.

The issue with distractions is that they keep us from focusing on what's important. This is expressively demonstrated in the story of Jesus' visit with two sisters named Mary and Martha:

> *"As Jesus and his disciples were on their way, he came to a village where a woman named Martha opened her home to him. She had a sister called Mary, who sat at the Lord's feet listening to what he said. But Martha was distracted by all the preparations that had to be made. She came to him and asked, 'Lord, don't you care that my sister has left me to do the work by myself? Tell her to help me!' 'Martha, Martha,' the Lord answered, 'you are worried and upset about many things, but only one thing is needed. Mary has chosen what is better, and it will not be taken away from her.'"*
> *-Luke 10:38-42 NIV*

Certainly the occasion necessitated preparation, but not at the expense of Martha's time with the Lord. The demands of the moment distracted Martha from what was most important in the moment. Sometimes we can get so caught up tending to things which demand our attention that we neglect the one thing that matters most. A visit from Jesus is an epic occurrence and presumably would be treated as such by anyone fortunate enough to experience it, but this example shows how easy it is to get our priorities mixed up once we become distracted. Yes, it was important to try and make Jesus' visit as nice as possible, but what was more important was to spend time with Him while He was there. Mary seized the moment, and in doing so she demonstrated how important it is not to allow anything to distract us from pursuing the presence of God.

When you live a distracted life you're busy but not accomplishing anything. You may exert a lot of effort on things, but at the end of the day you have nothing substantial to show for your time.

Two of the biggest distractions that many people grapple with are television and the internet.   Research shows that the average American watches 40 hours of television per week.   That's a considerable amount of time to spend on something that offers almost nothing in return. Yet, many of us allow television to consume hours of our day without ever considering what we give up in exchange for it. During the writing of this book, my top priority was to finish it in a timely manner.   Initially, I had great expectations; I had a plan, an outline and agreed to hold myself to a strict writing schedule. I was excited about this project and did not foresee any roadblocks to my success. However, when year six rolled around and I hadn't finished yet, I had to take an honest look at why. I sincerely felt that I didn't have any more time to devote to this book, other than the time that I had already allotted for it. But, in the spirit of honesty, I decided to audit my actions for a period of one week. I specifically focused on the amount of time that I spent on nonessential activities such as social media and game apps. To my surprise, I discovered that those things were consuming more of my time than what was appropriate. When I curtailed those activities I was able to add 3 hours of time back into each of my days.   That resulted in an additional 21 hours per week that I freed up to work on this book.

Some distractions are a normal part of life while others are gratuitous in nature and exist only to sideline our goals. Many distractions are intrusive, but some we actually invite upon ourselves. In my case, I allowed social media to consume time that would have been better spent elsewhere. When you have pressing goals it is prudent to limit non-essential   activities   because   they   quickly   become distractions that break your momentum. Once your momentum is lost it's extremely difficult to regain focus and get back on track. This is why it's crucial that we examine everything that either pulls us away or hinders us from focusing on our priorities. We must identify what is most important, respond accordingly, and always ensure that our choices support our goals. Life is all about choices; if we chose not to control our time it will slip away from us, and at the end of the day, our accomplishments will be few and far between.

Some people have cycles of inconsistency in their lives, never following through with what they say they will do. These types of people fail (at their goals) more often than they succeed because they lack discipline. There are also those whose lives are filled with so much clutter that they live in a perpetual state of confusion, unable to focus on one thing for any length of time. If you fall into either of these categories, realize that bad habits do not have power over you unless you allow them to. You have the ability to change but it will require more from you than you're currently giving. You will need to be single-minded and vigilant in order to conquer distractions, prioritize your life and live up to your full potential in God.

As you seek to develop and maintain a relationship with God, distractions will come from everywhere so you must purposefully protect your time with Him. Be flexible, but remain consistent; find a balance that works for you and manage your time wisely. If at any point you become too busy to spend time with God, it is a clear indicator that your priorities are out of order. It's very easy to allow the day-to-day issues of life to steal your time with God, but keep in mind, relationships cannot withstand continual neglect. Just as weeds can ruin a natural garden, repeated neglect can most certainly ruin your relationship with God.

✠   **Disappointment-** Disappointment is the feeling of

sorrow that is caused by unfulfilled expectations. This weed is like a leach; it attaches itself to you and attempts to suck the life out of your faith.

"Hope deferred makes the heart sick..." -Prov 13:12

Disappointment is a devastating emotion; it knocks the wind out of your sails and delivers a crushing blow to your spirit. It can defeat your hopes and cause you to give up on all of your dreams. Regardless of who you are, everyone experiences disappointment, and depending on the level of hurt the experience causes, it can be difficult to recover from. If we aren't careful, disappointment can make us walk out on God and never look back!

There are many experiences that can cause disappointment; divorce, failed relationships, betrayal, broken promises, loss of a loved one, being picked over for a job promotion, the list goes on and on. Being a Believer does not shield us from experiencing disappointment. Christians go through the same peaks and valleys as unbelievers do. The difference is, when an unbeliever experiences disappointment they tend to give up on life, but when a Believer experiences disappointment, they tend to give up on God. As Christians, our disappointment is oftentimes caused by undue expectations that we place on God. We anticipate that He'll do a specific thing in a certain way, and when He doesn't do what we expect, in the manner in which we expected, we become disappointed. Our disappointment then becomes an indictment against God; if He loves me why didn't He come through for me, why did He allow this to happen, how can He let me go through this much pain?

It is a mistake to believe that serving God means we'll always get what we want and that nothing bad will ever happen to us. If that were true, there would be no need for faith.   Most of us would not admit that we expect our relationship with God to always bring sunny days, but our response to disappointment oftentimes proves that we do. When we don't get the blessing we asked for, when our dreams fall apart at the seams or when our prayers go unanswered, we're ready to turn our backs on God and label our entire belief system a farce.

Every Christian goes through difficult times, but if we fail to prepare for them, when they come they will annihilate our faith.   God does not take pleasure in watching us suffer and He does not orchestrate bad things for us to go through, but we live in a fallen world so bad things are bound to happen.   The key is to hang on to your faith.   We may not always understand why we go through certain things, but we must learn to trust in the goodness of God.

Life is not perfect, but we serve a perfect God.   He is able to restore losses and bring something good out of every bad thing that we go through, but we must trust Him in the midst of our disappointment.   Trust Him even if it feels like He let you down.   Trust Him even if you're convinced He betrayed your trust.

The way to prepare for disappointment is to make up your mind that no matter what comes your way, you're going to worship through it.   When things don't go according to plan - worship.   When God does not do what you want Him to do - worship.   When life pulls the rug from underneath your feet - worship.   Worship through every disappointment, through every hard place, through every storm, through every test and through every trial.   Don't give up on God!

I have learned that if I don't worship through disappointment, my heart can quickly turn cold towards God; I may not verbally denounce Him but inwardly I turn away and don't want anything else to do with Him. This is a very dark place to be in and it leads to nowhere. Having rebounded from that place, I can attest to how crucial it is to worship through disappointment. Worshiping through disappointment anchors your faith in the Word and it is a profound declaration of your trust in God.

A couple of years ago I met a man who turned his back on God and renounced his faith. He had been a Christian for many years, had a strong relationship with the Lord and held a leadership position in a very well-known Ministry. After experiencing some difficult years in marriage, his wife filed for divorce. He loved her very much and did not want her to leave, so he prayed and asked God to save his marriage. He then put into practice every spiritual exercise that he learned through the years; he engaged in warfare prayers, fasted, recited faith confessions, attended relationship conferences – you name it, he did it. He even received a prophetic word that God was going to restore his marriage. The more he prayed, the more confident he became that God was going to answer his prayers. Sadly, however, after a period of separation, their divorce was finalized and his wife left him for good. She had determined that their marriage was unsalvageable and decided to move on with her life. Her decision sent him into an emotional tailspin; he became filled with rage and unrepentantly turned his back on God, vowing never to serve Him again. The sting of disappointment cast a dark shadow over his entire life. He became a recluse, isolated himself from all of his Christian friends and left the church. I offered to pray for him but he strongly rejected my offer and told me that he would never trust God again.

Disappointment is a temporary feeling so it's wise not to respond to it until the emotional dust settles. It's not always apparent why things don't turn out the way we hope or expect; but if we hold fast to our faith, sooner or later

God will reveal Himself in the situation. God may not always show us the "why" but He will always cause the outcome to work together for our good if we maintain our trust in Him (Romans 8:28). Disappointment never has the final say unless we choose to stop trusting in God. In the case with the divorced man, I think he gave up on God too soon; just because his wife divorced him did not mean that God couldn't restore their marriage. But sadly, he took things at face value and gave up on God.

When dealing with disappointment it is a common self-defense mechanism to try and protect ourselves from repeated emotional pain, so after experiencing disappointment in a certain area our guards go up and we vow never to repeat that scenario again. This type of behavior is crippling and can rob us of our future. Several years ago, I became stagnant on my job and began looking for ways to advance my career. During that time, an opportunity became available that piqued my interest; it wasn't my dream job but it was definitely a step in the right direction. Initially, I wasn't sure whether I was going to apply for the position or not, but during my indecision, four people approached me, on four different occasions, and suggested that I apply for the job. Two out of those four people were senior level executives. Naturally, with that type of support I decided to apply for the job. Shortly after applying, I was granted an interview. It was one of the best interviews I ever had; I was confident, poised and said all of the right things. I was positive that I aced the interview and would soon be contacted with the job offer. I was so excited, I walked around all day praising and thanking God for the new door He was opening for me. I was on cloud nine because it appeared that things were finally coming together for me.

The next week I had a follow-up meeting with the hiring manager and what I thought would be good news ended up being very disappointing news. To my dismay, I was told that I didn't get the job. It was all I could do to maintain my composure as tears began welling up in my eyes. When I got home that evening I fell apart. I felt sucker punched by God. I felt like He set me up to look like a fool. Why would He allow senior level executives to encourage me to apply for a job that He knew I was not going to get? My questions went unanswered, so I tucked away my disappointment and went back to business as usual.

Less than one month later, low and behold, a posting went up for a position that was my actual "dream job." I stumbled upon it by accident, but after reading through the job description, I discovered that it was the exact opportunity that I had always wanted and hoped would one day come along. Surprisingly, however, I immediately decided not to apply for the job because I didn't want to go through anymore disappointment. So I pretended as if I never saw the posting and went back to my daily grind.

Two weeks later, on the day that the posting was set to come down, I was encouraged to apply for the job through a chance encounter with a peer. So, with less than 30 minutes left in the work-day, I submitted my application. Unbeknownst to me, the hiring manager wanted someone who had completed our company's internal development program. Ironically, I had just finished the program, and I was the only applicant who met this particular requirement. In a nutshell, I interviewed for the job, and shortly thereafter, I was offered the position. Amazing! I didn't see this coming! The job was literally mine before I ever applied for it, but I almost missed it because I was busy nursing my wounds and afraid of being disappointed again.

Understand that trust in God will always require active faith. If you sit on the sidelines of life fearing disappointment, you will miss your blessing every time.

We have to realize that God is always on our side and whether we perceive it or not, He always wants to do good things for us. I was disappointed because I didn't get what I wanted, but all along, God had a better plan. If I would have gotten the first job that I applied for, I would have missed the real blessing that God had for me.

When disappointment strikes, don't allow it to eclipse your faith, because God is able to take anything that we go through and cause it to work out for our good. Even if the situation is your fault, God is not surprised by your mistakes. When we mess up and miss out on His blessings, He lovingly begins working out a plan to restore back to us what we lost. This is why we can trust God in the face of every disappointment, because He is good and His mercy endures forever.

Worshiping *through* disappointment is the most effective way to keep this weed from latching on to you and stealing your faith. Similar to other weeds, this one can spring up at any time so we must always be prepared to deal with it at a moment's notice. When disappointment rears its ugly head, pull out your worship.

✟ **Discouragement-** Discouragement means to lose confidence and become disheartened. Discouragement is very much akin to disappointment. These two weeds typically grow together, feeding off of each other and fueling one another's strength. If you don't uproot disappointment from your garden, discouragement will spring up and the two of them together will be twice as hard to get rid of. The difference between disappointment and discouragement is disappointment is an immediate reaction to a single negative event, whereas discouragement is an outlook that develops over time due to a series of negative experiences or an ongoing negative circumstance.

Discouragement hovers over you like a dark cloud and follows you around wherever you go. It steals your joy and causes you to view life through a negative lens. It hits you with a barrage of depressing emotions and leaves you feeling mentally spent. When you're discouraged, you lose your will to worship.

No one is immune to discouragement, rich, poor, black, white, sinner, saint; it happens to everyone. Discouragement is one of the biggest obstacles that most people will face in life.

Discouragement can be caused by a host of things, namely repeated disappointment, extended seasons of difficulty, failure to accomplish goals, illness, unanswered prayer, and delayed expectations. When discouragement sets in, you develop a pessimistic attitude and become convinced that you'll never get what you want out of life.

Discouragement is one of the enemy's most diabolical weapons and he wields it against Believers for the express purpose of stealing our destiny. If he can get us to lose confidence in God's plan for our lives, we will lose our expectation for the future. Once our expectation is gone, we have nothing left to hope for. Hope is like oxygen to the soul, without it, we die. No one can live without hope!

As Christians, we're most vulnerable to discouragement when we're waiting on a promise from God to be fulfilled. When God makes us a promise, whether it's a written promise in His Word or a personal promise revealed to us by His spirit, there is usually a waiting period from when the promise is made to when it actually comes to pass. The waiting period can be a short amount of time or a long duration of time, and the longer you wait, the more susceptible you are to becoming discouraged. A married couple waiting on the promise of a child, for example, may grow discouraged as the years pass, fearing they'll miss their window of opportunity to be able to conceive a baby. The longer they wait, the more it looks as if they're running out of time, so they begin to lose hope and question God's timing. Long-term waiting periods are not meant to be punitive, but God has a set time for when He will bring His promises to pass in our lives; and even if it takes a long time, His timing is always perfect. Usually, however, we cannot appreciate God's timing until we get to the finish line and see the full picture. Only then do we realize why we had to wait.

Waiting on God will transform you and prepare you to walk in your promise; whether you're waiting to be promoted, get married, conceive a child, or start your own ministry, God will take you through a process to train and develop you to successfully handle your promise. Without preparation, failure is inevitable.

David had to wait more than 15 years after he was anointed king before he began to reign, and he spent most of that time running for his life. He was in very adverse conditions, but that was all a part of God's training process to prepare him to become a great king. While on the run, David built a successful army out of inexperienced, distressed men, he became a master strategist, acquired effective leadership skills and learned how to efficiently manage resources. All of these abilities served him well when he became king, but they came at a price–waiting on God. There were many times when David felt abandoned and afflicted in his soul, but he managed to defeat discouragement by pressing into his relationship with God.

In ¹Samuel 30, David and his army had left their camp at Ziklag en route to fight a battle, and while they were gone an army of Amalekites came and raided their camp. The Amalekites captured all of their possessions and took their wives and children hostage. When David and his army returned to Ziklag and realized what happened, they became grief-stricken and inconsolable. The Bible says that they "wept until they had no more strength to weep."

This, in and of itself, was a devastating situation to go through, but things got much worse for David. As a result of this attack, his entire army turned on him and wanted to kill him.

> *"David was greatly distressed, for the men spoke of stoning him because the souls of them all were bitterly grieved, each man for his sons and daughters..." -1Samuel 30:6 AMP*

If there was ever a moment in David's 15-year journey when discouragement could have defeated him, this was the moment. On top of being unjustifiably hunted and forced to live as a fugitive, this attack stripped him of everything that he had, including the respect of his brigade—the very men who he mentored and trained to be successful.

But look at what David did next...

> *"...David encouraged himself in the LORD his God." -1Samuel 30:6*

Instead of engaging in self-pity and allowing discouragement to take over, David encouraged himself in the Lord. While this verse does not give specific details about David's response, David wrote many psalms that corresponded with events in his life, so we know enough about him to conclude that he encouraged himself with statements such as; "Why are you cast down, O my soul? And why are you disquieted within me? Hope in God, for I shall yet praise Him..." (Psalms 42:5) There is no doubt that David used praise as a means to counter the onslaught of discouragement.

David then asked God should he go after the men responsible for the attack. God answered him and said; "Pursue, for you shall surely overtake them and without fail recover all." (1 Samuel 30:8) So David and his army went after the Amalekites and everything happened just as God said it would; "David recovered all that the Amalekites had taken and rescued his two wives. Nothing was missing, small or great, sons or daughters, spoil or anything that had been taken; David recovered all." (1 Samuel 30:18-19)

What's most interesting to note is that David became king right after the battle at Ziklag. His 15-year waiting period culminated at the juncture of this disastrous event, and his destiny was left hanging in the balance. If David had allowed discouragement to set in, he would have sank into despair and lost all hope -- and that is where his story would have ended. Instead, he defeated discouragement, came out of the attack unscathed and stepped right into his God-ordained destiny.

When you hit a wall, when everything seems to fall apart or when you feel as if your promise will never come to pass; encourage yourself in the Lord. Call to memory all of the trials that God faithfully brought you through, and then lift up your voice and praise Him; praise Him for who He is, praise Him for what He's done and praise Him for what He will do. Praise defeats discouragement one hundred percent of the time but we must tap into it; we cannot just sit idly by and wait for discouragement to pass us over. If we don't fight it off, it will hold us in its grip and eventually destroy our lives.

Discouragement is a strategic attack designed to hit us at critical stages in our journey. There is usually more to discouragement than meets the eye so it's vital that we refuse to succumb to it. David didn't know that his destiny was at stake when the Amalekites attacked his camp, but if he hadn't beat discouragement at that point it would have cost him his breakthrough. Likewise, we don't know what's at stake when discouragement comes against us, so it's vitally important that we respond to it correctly.

Discouragement knocks at everyone's door, but it's a choice whether or not to let it in. If you choose to let it in, it will settle into your soul and fill your entire life with despair. Your days will be spent wallowing in self-pity, frustrated with everything and everyone. You'll wake up sad and go to bed angry. Before long, you'll develop a victim mentality and begin looking for others to appease you. This sad cycle will perpetuate itself until you make the choice to overcome discouragement. Until you choose to exercise power over it, discouragement will continually defeat you.

Battling discouragement is not easy, but it's a fight we must take on. The thing to remember is that the feeling of discouragement is always an attack from the enemy; it's never just an innocent mood swing, it's a tactical aggressive attempt to annihilate your faith. When discouragement strikes, it packs a mean punch and hits you with a slew of negative emotions: discontent, disgust, impatience, indifference, anger, sorrow, unhappiness, dissatisfaction..., the list goes on. These emotions gnaw at your psyche until you reach a point where you give up and lose hope. So many Christians have folded under the pressures of life because they chose not to fight against discouragement; but it didn't have to be so. Discouragement cannot defeat Believers if we fight against it. All we have to do is utilize the weapons that God gave us and fight against the enemy. If we fight, we will win.

"Resist the devil, and he will flee from you."
-James 4:7

How do you defend yourself when discouragement strikes? You *resist* it. To resist means: refuse to accept; refuse to go along with; refuse to give in to. You have to refuse to become discouraged about your situation. When the negative emotions start to come against you, head them off at the pass. Speak to them with authority and let them know that you reject their influence in your life. If you stand your ground, you will win and the negative emotions will cease. The only individuals who fail to beat discouragement are those who do not fight against it. If you fight, you will win, as long as you stand your ground.

You don't have to fight the battle alone, enlist the help of a prayer partner to fight along with you, or seek counsel from church members in leadership roles. Do whatever you need to do to get free and stay free, because there's a lot at stake.

If you chose not to fight against discouragement you become open prey for the enemy, and like a vulture, he'll pick at you until there's nothing left. Understand that the enemy wants to keep you from making it to your finish line, so you must counter discouragement at all costs. It doesn't matter how long you've been waiting, it doesn't matter how far you've strayed from your life's purpose, it doesn't matter how many times you've blown it, it doesn't even matter how many times you've missed it. God is faithful and He will do what He promised to do in your life. But you must trust Him and refuse to become discouraged, even when it appears like everything is against you. Nothing that opposes you is stronger than Almighty God, and if He is for you, who or what can stand against you?

Discouraged people do not have the will to worship; they only want to sulk in misery and wait for their situation to change. That is the problem with this weed; it steals your motivation to tend your garden. Once you let your garden go to waste, your relationship with God diminishes and your life becomes a dry place. This is why it's so important to remove this weed as swiftly as possible, because it's not worth jeopardizing the relationship you've built with God. Do your part to keep this weed at bay and you'll enjoy a harvest of enduring intimacy with the Lord.

Tending a garden is not easy work; you're in the hot sun for hours at a time, shoveling dirt, uprooting weeds, making sure all of your plants get enough water...etc, it is a very laborious process. But the end result is so rewarding, the gardener willingly does whatever is necessary to maintain their garden. Ministering to God is not laborious, it is a joy, but if you want a healthy lifelong relationship with Him, it will require spiritual work. You will have to be disciplined, motivated and committed, and you'll have to hold yourself accountable for all of your choices. If you do the spiritual work, the end result will be a rewarding relationship that will stand the test of time.

I drove through a neighborhood yesterday and saw several yards that were overgrown with weeds. The weeds had grown so wild, they left no trace of what was there before. In direct contrast, this tree-lined street also included elegant homes with perfectly manicured lawns and beautiful flower beds that dazzled the eyes. All of a sudden, I was struck by how this disparity clearly relates to our relationship with God. Neglected gardens are unattractive to gaze upon and impossible to keep hidden. Eventually, if you fail to tend your relationship with God, the consequences are present in almost every area of your life. You'll look around for the joy you once had but discover it's no longer there. Left in its place is a life that's become chaotic and unfruitful. Peace eludes you and challenges seem insurmountable. Before long, you realize that your life has become a dry and desolate place.

Whenever I stray from God and neglect my garden, I feel like a child hiding from my parent after committing an infraction -- tiptoeing around, fearful of getting in trouble. Inwardly, I think I'm getting away with something, but in reality I'm creating a wasteland that I will eventually have to walk through. God does not want our lives to be filled with desolation and despair; He wants us to be filled with the joy and fulfillment that comes from spending time in His presence. The most breathtaking moments of my life have been the moments I've spent in the presence of the Lord; when it's just Him and I alone together. Nothing compares to the joy of being with God, it is a level of joy that is far beyond our human ability to produce.

> *"You will show me the path of life; in Your presence is fullness of joy, at Your right hand there are pleasures forevermore." -Psalms 16:11 AMP*

Summary

The most important relationship we will ever have is our relationship with God. Knowing God intimately is the key that causes us to thrive in our Christian walk. When we take the time to worship God, we cultivate a connection with Him that is second to none. The most worthwhile investment we can make in life is to spend quality time in the presence of God.

Action Point:

1.   Ask God to show you the things in your life that draw you away from Him and keep you from knowing Him more.

Sometimes we unwittingly give unimportant issues top priority in our lives and fail to allocate any time to focus on God. For this reason, we each must seek God's wisdom for how to prioritize our lives so that we're able to spend regular time with Him.

Pray this prayer:

Dear Heavenly Father, I want to embark on a worship journey with You, and I want to know You like never before. I trust You to chart the course that I must travel and I will cling to You through every peak and valley. Bind my feet to the path You set before me and remove everything that would cause me to stumble and lose ground. If I ever stray away from You, correct my course and put me back on track. Help me to identify the things that jeopardize my commitment to You, and help me to diligently seek Your face. Teach me how to tend my worship garden so that I can keep the weeds out. When disappointments come, help me to trust you and worship through them. When discouragement knocks at my door, show me how to resist it and maintain my passion and desire for You.   Fix my eyes upon Your glory so that You're all I see and all I want. As I draw near to You, I remove the mask, the make-up and the façade, and I give you the real me. Thank you for loving me unconditionally, in Jesus name, Amen.

An Invitation

If the concepts in this book are new to you, then perhaps you haven't been introduced to Jesus Christ. The Bible teaches that the only way to enjoy a relationship with God is *through* His son Jesus Christ. *"Jesus said to him, 'I am the way, the truth, and the life. No one comes to the Father except through Me.'"* (John 14:6 NKJV) Jesus gives us access to the presence of God and the blessings of God, but we must first accept Him as Lord and Savoir of our lives. Regardless of your past and what you may have done, God loves you and He wants a relationship with you. He sent His son into the world to save you from sin and destruction. *"For God so loved the world that He gave His only begotten Son, that whoever believes in Him should not perish but have everlasting life."* (John 3:16 NKJV) Jesus laid down His life for you so that you can spend eternity with Him in heaven and experience God's best here on earth. If you would like to receive Jesus into your life, pray the following prayer out loud from your heart:

> *Heavenly Father, I come to You admitting that I am a sinner. Right now, I choose to turn away from sin, and I ask You to cleanse me of all unrighteousness. I believe that Your Son, Jesus, died on the cross to take away my sins. I also believe that He rose again from the dead so that I might be forgiven of my sins and made righteous through faith in Him. I call upon the name of Jesus Christ and confess Him to be the Savior and Lord of my life. Jesus, I choose to follow You and ask that You fill me with the power of the Holy Spirit. I declare that right now I am a child of God. I am free from sin and full of the righteousness of God. I am saved in Jesus' name, Amen!*

Welcome to the family of God! It's important to follow-up your salvation prayer by joining a church. Regular church attendance will help you learn and grow and prosper in your new faith. If you don't know where to go, research your local churches and pray for God to lead you to the church that He desires for you to join.

Made in the USA
Middletown, DE
12 May 2022

65673664R00094